READING
to **LEARN**
in Secondary Classrooms

We dedicate this book to our families and friends, especially Leta Jo Maue and her husband, Fred, who started all this. We especially dedicate this book to hard-working teachers everywhere.

READING
to LEARN
in Secondary Classrooms

INCREASING COMPREHENSION
AND UNDERSTANDING

Daniel M. Perna   Sarah F. Mahurt

CORWIN
A SAGE Company

For information:

 Corwin
A SAGE Company
2455 Teller Road
Thousand Oaks, California 91320
(800) 233-9936
Fax: (800) 417-2466
www.corwinpress.com

SAGE Ltd.
1 Oliver's Yard
55 City Road
London EC1Y 1SP
United Kingdom

SAGE India Pvt. Ltd.
B 1/I 1 Mohan Cooperative
    Industrial Area
Mathura Road, New Delhi 110 044
India

SAGE Asia-Pacific Pte. Ltd.
33 Pekin Street #02-01
Far East Square
Singapore 048763

Printed in the United States of America.

Library of Congress Cataloging-in-Publication Data

Perna, Daniel M.
Reading to learn in secondary classrooms : increasing comprehension and understanding / Daniel M. Perna and Sarah F. Mahurt.
    p. cm.
Includes bibliographical references and index.
ISBN 978-1-4129-5611-6 (cloth)
ISBN 978-1-4129-5612-3 (pbk.)
    1. Reading (Secondary) 2. Reading comprehension. I. Mahurt, Sarah F. II. Title.

LB1632.P395 2009
428.4071'2—dc22   2009004911

This book is printed on acid-free paper.

09 10 11 12 13 10 9 8 7 6 5 4 3 2 1

Acquisitions Editor:	Cathy Hernandez
Editorial Assistant:	Sarah Bartlett
Production Editor:	Jane Haenel
Copy Editor:	Jenifer Dill
Typesetter:	C&M Digitals (P) Ltd.
Proofreader:	Theresa Kay
Indexer:	Sylvia Coates
Cover and Graphic Designer:	Michael Dubowe

Contents

List of Figures and Tables

FIGURES

TABLES

Preface

Because of the increased demands for literacy in the workplace and in higher education, secondary students today need to be more highly literate than ever before. At the same time, teachers are saying that students find reading difficult and don't complete reading assignments in school. In addition, the level of difficulty in content textbooks and of technical writing is beyond that found in literature books, the traditional place where reading skills are developed. Jacobs (1999) stated that "texts used in subject areas often employ language, syntax, vocabulary, and concepts that are specific to a particular field of study. Merely assigning reading does not help students learn how to tangle with these specialized texts to construct meaning; teachers must help prepare students for and guide them through the texts so that they will learn from them most effectively" (p. 1). Thus, secondary content-area teachers must have instructional strategies to help students read within the context of their subject.

The idea for this book grew from our observations of secondary classrooms where students were not engaged by their reading. Because of our belief that reading is the core of any subject-matter learning, we decided to write a book that could help secondary teachers. We found many resources available that focused on content literacy and felt that a book that concentrated on only a few of the many content-literacy approaches would be more manageable for teachers. We wanted the book to be user-friendly and filled with examples from classrooms where teachers were using instructional strategies that not only helped students increase their ability to read complex texts, but also helped them learn more about the content being taught and engaged their interest.

In Chapter 1, we review the state of adolescent literacy today and the need for literacy in the twenty-first century. We outline some of the research as well as look at a lifelong view of literacy growth—rather than one that stops with elementary school—and demonstrate what it is that proficient readers do.

Chapter 2 gives an overview of the instructional process that is explained in more detail in the rest of the book. It includes two detailed lesson plans that show how an English teacher and a science teacher engaged students before, during, and after reading assignments.

Chapter 3 goes into detail about the before-reading practices that teachers can use to prepare students for reading. These before-reading activities highlight the importance of background knowledge as well as ways to set a purpose for reading. Vocabulary development before reading is also discussed in this chapter.

In Chapter 4, we move to ways to actively engage students in their reading. Different ways to guide students' thinking while reading are included. We also caution teachers about the use of oral reading in secondary classrooms.

In Chapter 5, we discuss activities that can be done after reading to solidify student learning and increase comprehension. The importance of writing is stressed, as is the use of graphic organizers for structuring learning.

Chapter 6 ties together the need for instructional strategies around reading in all secondary classrooms and the needs of today's students. It also brings assessment to the forefront of instructional decision making.

The Appendix in this book outlines the process we went through in developing the format of the instructional strategies outline, and teachers were able to use the strategies in ways that improved student achievement.

We hope this book will support secondary teachers as they work to improve learning in their content area as well as improve students' reading ability. We understand the challenges teachers face and want this book to assist with those challenges.

Acknowledgments

We want to acknowledge the following schools that gave us the opportunity to work closely with their entire high school faculty in the process of developing this concept: the director, Cosmas Curry, the administration, and the faculty of the Columbia-Montour Area Vocational Technical School in Bloomsburg, Pennsylvania; and the superintendent, Cheryl Pataky, and the administration and faculty of the Moshannon Valley School District in Houtzdale, Pennsylvania.

We extend a special thank you and acknowledgment to Jennifer Taylor, a student at Columbia-Montour Area Vocational-Technical School in Bloomsburg, Pennsylvania. Miss Taylor draws pictures for Mr. Marty Christian, and we used one of her pictures in this book.

We want to acknowledge the following educators, who offered ideas and assistance in the development of lessons that they employed in their classrooms: Michelle Bonser and Jack Moyer of the Monroe County Career and Technology Center in Bartonsville, PA; Tim Deshem of Greenwood High School in Millerstown, PA; David Garnes of Tussey Mountain High School in Saxton, PA; Susan Hetrick of Hughesville High School in Hughesville, PA; Eric Bergmueller of Milton Area School District in Milton, PA; Cheri Long of Selinsgrove Area High School in Selinsgrove, PA; Chris Neff of Shikellamy School District in Sunbury, PA; Lisa Strickland, Gail Parsons, Elaine Saladyga, Nicole Fink, Timothy Mauk, Robert Marino, David Wolinsky, Terry Sheaffer, Marty Christian, Rick Miles, Donna Harris, Michelle Twiddy, and Steven Shadel of the Columbia-Montour Area Vocational-Technical School; and Joseph Holenchik, Tom Webb, Thomas Boito, and Kristi Buell of the Moshannon Valley School District in Houtzdale, PA.

Publisher's Acknowledgments

Corwin gratefully acknowledges the contributions of the following reviewers:

Joan Baltezore, Biology Teacher
West Fargo High School
West Fargo, ND

Ellen E. Coulson, US History Teacher
Sig Rogich Middle School
Las Vegas, NV

Darron Laughland, English Teacher
Kennet High School
Conway, NH

Sandra Ness, Literacy Teacher
Patrick Henry High School
Minneapolis, MN

About the Authors

 **Daniel M. Perna** is a consultant working with schools and businesses concerning twenty-first-century educational issues. Dan spent thirty-three years in public education as a school principal, district assistant superintendent, athletic director, basketball coach, and English teacher. He has written professional articles and has published one professional book, *Aligning Standards and Curriculum for Classroom Success*. The book was honored by the Pennsylvania Association for Supervision and Curriculum Directors in 2002 with its research and publication award.

Dan is noted for his motivational keynote speeches concerning rigorous academics integrated with technology education. He has presented over two hundred workshops and conferences in seventeen states and in Canada. Much of his professional development work has been done in Pennsylvania, where he has focused on how to implement academic standards in a process leading to a stronger merger of assessment and instruction.

Dan is an adjunct professor with the Graduate School of Teacher Education at Wilkes University and a doctoral advisor for Nova Southeastern University. He has served on committees with the Pennsylvania Association of Supervision and Curriculum Directors and is a past executive board member of the Pennsylvania Staff Development Council.

Sarah F. Mahurt has more than thirty years of experience as an educator. In that time, she has worked as a classroom teacher, reading specialist, university professor, and district administrator with a focus on improving instruction and student achievement.

Sarah's recent publications include a book titled *Building Bridges From Primary to Intermediate Literacy* and an article on the integration of reading and writing. She has also made national and international presentations on children's literature, literacy teaching and learning, and school reform in literacy education. She has consulted with numerous schools and districts across the country. She chaired a committee to develop a statewide network of educators in Indiana focused on improving writing instruction.

Sarah is currently the director of Curriculum, Assessment, and Technology for the Virgin Islands Department of Education, St. Croix District. She recently served as professor of Literacy and Language Education at Purdue University and director of the Purdue Literacy Network. She has received several honors, including the Purdue University Department of Curriculum and Instruction's Engagement Award for developing school reform efforts. She has received the Celebrate Literacy Award from the St. Croix Chapter of the International Reading Association and the Teaching Excellence Award at the University of the Virgin Islands.

1

Introduction

Today, secondary teachers face many challenges. They feel over-whelmed by the number of students they teach, the range of abilities in their classes, the pressure of high-stakes assessments, and No Child Left Behind (NCLB) requirements. There are also constraints of time and space that impact teaching in secondary schools. Students move through the day, often in short blocks of time, to classrooms that are set up for specific purposes: lab tables in science or individual seats facing the chalkboards in math (Moje, 2006). All of these constraints make it difficult for secondary teachers to feel that they have the expertise or the time to teach their content knowledge *and* literacy.

In addition, many secondary teachers have had workshop sessions on topics such as "Writing Across the Curriculum" and "Every Teacher a Teacher of Reading" where they developed the distinct notion that they were expected to become teachers of reading and writing. Most secondary teachers have not been formally trained to be teachers of reading and writing; they were taught to be content-specific experts. They have been expected to focus only on their particular content and to impart that knowledge to their students. For many secondary teachers, literacy competencies are skills they expect students to have in place prior to coming to secondary school. From this viewpoint, students were to have learned how to read in elementary school, so a focus on reading in secondary content classrooms should be unnecessary. Thus, over the years, many secondary teachers have not embraced the idea of bringing literacy instruction into their content area (Moje, 2006).

We understand the difficulties faced by secondary teachers today and hope this book will provide some direction for the increasingly important role they play in developing adolescent literacy. We take the stance that it is important to develop students as *learners* rather than just as readers or writers. It is the content teacher's focus to help students learn the ways of knowing, doing, and communicating in that content area (Moje, 2006) while also teaching specific content.

In the book *The World Is Flat*, Friedman (2006) refers to two ideas that are important in the development of adolescents and relate directly to our learning stance. The first is that students must learn to work hard and accept the realities of needing to work hard in order to succeed. Second, Friedman believes that the best teachers and schools teach students how to learn and to continue learning throughout life. This means that secondary schools must focus on literacy as a learning tool that will help students develop their ability to be creative and innovative thinkers. Teachers and students must see literacy as a catalyst for learning how to learn new and different concepts— important in a fast-changing world.

The state of adolescent literacy is seen as in crisis today (Graham & Perin, 2007; Heller & Greenleaf, 2007; National Association of State Boards of Education [NASBE], 2006). According to international assessments (Organization for Economic Co-operation and Development [OECD], 2003), fifteen-year-olds in the United States rank fifteenth in the world and are below the international average for engagement in reading and school. Data from the National Assessment of Educational Progress (NAEP) show that one-third of the country's secondary students are proficient in reading, while only 3% of eighth graders and 5% of twelfth graders read at an advanced level. There has been little progress toward improving achievement at the secondary level on this assessment to match the growth seen in fourth-grade results (Perie, Grigg, & Donahue, 2005). While most adolescents do have basic reading skills and strategies in place and can answer basic comprehension questions, few have developed the more advanced ability to interpret, synthesize, and critique expository texts (Balfanz, McPartland, & Shaw, 2002; Moje, 2006).

Writing proficiency is also seen as in crisis in national reports (Graham & Perin, 2007). According to the 2002 NAEP results, gains were made in eighth-grade writing between 1998 and 2002, with 15% below basic and 31% proficient or advanced. The performance of twelfth graders was mixed. In 2002, 26% of twelfth graders were below basic, an increase of those below the standard. However, 24% were proficient or advanced in 2002, a gain of 2% from 1998. While most adolescents can complete basic writing with acceptable form, content, and language usage, they cannot produce high-quality writing with the complex language and thought necessary for future success (National Commission on Writing, 2006).

While the growth of literacy development in the United States appears to be stagnant at the secondary level, the need for higher levels of literacy to function in the workplace and in life is increasing. Advanced levels of literacy will be needed not only for successful job performance but also for running households, acting as citizens in a democratic society, and coping with everyday life (Friedman, 2006; Heller & Greenleaf, 2007; Moore, Bean, Birdyshaw, & Rycik, 1999). Young people today will need "sophisticated literacy skills to negotiate a rapidly changing global and knowledge-based economy" (NASBE, 2006, p. 8) to live and work in the twenty-first century. Basic levels of literacy proficiency will not be enough. In the report of the New Commission on the Skills of the American Workforce (National Center on Education and the Economy [NCEE], 2007), commission members state that an essential foundation for success in the workplace of the future will include high levels of preparation in reading, writing, speaking, mathematics, science, literature, history, and the arts. This clearly indicates that schools must prepare students to learn how to comprehend material across all areas of the curriculum. What is not so clear is who should do this and how it will get done.

For several decades, content literacy instruction has been researched and presented to both preservice and inservice content-area teachers as specific strategies to gain information from text (Moje, 2006). Research has also found that many secondary teachers are not convinced that they need to teach reading strategies; rather, they feel they should concentrate on the subject matter of their content area. Many feel that adding literacy instruction as part of their teaching would be time consuming and better left to others. Because secondary teacher preparation has focused on content knowledge, there needs to be a clear understanding of which aspects of literacy are the responsibility of each content area. Teachers need to be encouraged to see that teaching adolescents the literacy strategies necessary for *their* content would develop a deeper understanding and a stronger learning of the content they are teaching. There is a need for secondary teachers to see the intersection of their content knowledge and the pedagogy specific to that content so they can help adolescents develop the advanced literacy skills they will need as well as give them a strong knowledge base (Heller & Greenleaf, 2007).

There are many recommendations from various sources that tell schools ways to improve adolescent literacy, and many feel there is a crisis in adolescent literacy development. However, there has not been the same widespread, systematic focus on developing literacy in secondary schools and districts as has been seen at the elementary level—especially regarding reading in the content areas and developing higher-level reading ability (Heller & Greenleaf, 2007; Meltzer, Smith, & Clark, 2001; NASBE, 2006). In the past, responses to educational crises have led to the idea that there are quick fixes to literacy issues, with programs being developed and sold as the way to fix the problem. However, there are no quick fixes (Allington, 1995; Alvermann, 2001; Tovani, 2004), but rather a need to mobilize the community, parents, teachers, and students for the hard work needed to improve adolescent literacy.

Many experts feel that secondary schools should take a comprehensive approach to literacy improvement whereby struggling readers receive specialized instruction from highly qualified literacy professionals and content teachers who provide instruction in the higher-level literacy development needed in their respective content areas (Biancarosa & Snow, 2004; Graham & Perin, 2007; Heller & Greenleaf, 2007; Moore et al., 1999; NASBE, 2006). This comprehensive approach should include attention to engagement and motivation, determination of the literacy demands in each content area, ongoing professional development, a focus on critical analysis of print and electronic media, and active student involvement in their own learning (Alvermann, 2001; Heller & Greenleaf, 2007; Moje, 2006). We understand the importance of the comprehensive approach; however, this book will focus on guiding secondary teachers to teach literacy processes in content areas with a focus on learning within that subject area. Our definition of literacy includes the idea that literacy is a tool for learning in any subject.

Because of the focus on high-stakes testing through the No Child Left Behind Act, teachers are concerned about how students will perform on standardized assessments. We believe that if students learn how to process information effectively and learn how to learn, they will also raise their achievement test scores (Wiggins & McTighe, 2005). For this to happen, secondary teachers may have to take a different perspective on literacy—one that is directly related to their content area. They may need to see literacy instruction as a learning tool that will help them instruct students in their respective content areas. If literacy teaching methods are going to succeed in secondary schools, teachers will need to envision that they are helping students comprehend the content in their respective curriculum, thereby becoming a more effective teacher. In addition, secondary teachers need to understand literacy development as a lifelong process, not something that ends in elementary school. This life-span development perspective provides a base for the importance of continuing literacy instruction in secondary schools and throughout the content areas (Alexander, 2005/2006).

Lifelong Literacy Growth and Development

It is important to understand that literacy development grows throughout life and that new learning must take place to meet different and increasingly difficult demands for literacy as children move from the elementary grades to secondary schools. Learning to read is a process that continues throughout life (Alexander, 2005/2006; RAND, 2002). Alexander (2005/2006) went so far as to state that "until we adopt this lifelong perspective, we continue to run the risk of turning out undeveloped, unmotivated, and uncritical readers unable to fulfill their responsibilities within a democratic society" (p. 413). To extend the idea of literacy beyond the basic development of reading acquisition seen in an elementary-school perspective, reading acquisition should be considered only as an initial step to becoming a proficient adult reader.

What does this development process look like? Proficient adult readers read for interest and pleasure in a variety of materials for a variety of purposes and are willing to work hard to understand material that is not easy to understand nor particularly interesting to them (RAND, 2002). This developmental perspective includes the idea that teachers must not only help students develop the strategic processes that allow adolescents to access text, but teachers must also develop students' background knowledge, vocabulary, understanding of purpose, and self-motivation and efficacy for when the going gets difficult. Additionally, teachers need to develop students' understanding of how textual material is put together and how this understanding guides the reader. These aspects of literacy change as the challenges of more complex content and higher expectations for deeper understanding grow across the years of schooling. There are developmental changes that occur as readers move from early reading, where novices are processing texts for basic understandings, to becoming proficient or expert readers who use a high degree of knowledge about reading processes and texts as well as strong background knowledge in a variety of areas. The basic processes for proficient readers are unconscious and automatic. This allows them to devote mental energy to synthesizing what they are reading and learning in order to become analytical and critical readers. These are the goals for secondary readers. In order to reach those goals, adolescents must continue to receive instruction in higher-level comprehending strategies, questioning techniques, and vocabulary development, as well as in the development and use of background knowledge. Table 1.1 outlines some aspects of literacy growth that can be seen as young people

Table 1.1   Changes Over Time in Literacy Development

Elementary School	Secondary School
Reading • Recognizes and accurately uses a large core of known words • Navigates texts subconsciously • Maintains deep understanding of text • Reads for extended periods of time and reads texts over several days • Responds to text both verbally and in writing • Monitors reading efficiently and able to flexibly problem solve without losing momentum or meaning • Is familiar with a wide variety of genres • Reads expressively in meaningful phrases with natural sounding fluency • Reads in specific areas of interest	**Reading** • Maintains areas of expertise from previous learning and experiences • Reads fluently both silently and orally • Applies knowledge of content domains while reading in a variety of texts • Applies knowledge of reading process while reading a variety of texts • Expands reading beyond specific areas of interest • Thinks about own understanding and self-regulates • Makes connections, interprets and synthesizes information read • Critiques texts and uses knowledge to determine authenticity
Writing • Makes deliberate decisions about form and genre • Writes longer pieces of several pages • Uses more complex sentence structures • Uses most end punctuation correctly; uses others variably (i.e., quotation marks, commas, ellipses) • Writes fluently, yet slows for difficult words • Spells most words correctly • Revises and edits	**Writing** • Maintains writing fluency • Revises for meaning, organization, audience, and purpose • Revises to use more specific language attending to tone, voice, and style • Edits pieces for grammar and mechanics attending to complex structures and punctuation • Understands audience and purpose and adjusts writing as needed

Elementary School	Secondary School
• Gives feedback for revision to other writers • Plans writing • Is forming a sense of audience	• Uses aspects of writers' craft from reading • Critically analyzes own and others' writing
Word Knowledge • Has basic phonics under control • Understands structural analysis of words including affixes, root and base words, and multisyllabic words • Has high frequency words under control in both reading and writing tasks • Uses visual analysis and understanding of word structure in spelling • Refines and extends vocabulary	**Word Knowledge** • Problem solves a wide variety of words while reading • Uses resources as needed for word solving and for meaning • Acquires vocabulary knowledge through reading • Uses more diverse vocabulary in writing • Produces carefully edited pieces with attention to spelling

Source: Adapted from Alexander, 2005/2006; Fountas & Pinnell, 2001; Mahurt, Metcalfe, & Gwyther, 2007.

move from the elementary grades to the secondary grades. This table can help teachers see where students need to be in order to be successful in high school and beyond, knowing that learners enter secondary schools at different places along a developmental continuum.

What to Teach

Before thinking about literacy practices in content area classrooms, teachers must first think about student engagement and motivation. Secondary teachers may say that students aren't motivated, yet the main method of instruction in secondary classrooms is the transmission model, which requires little student participation (Alvermann, 2001; Moje, 2006). The transmission model sets up a passive learning stance in students that is often not engaging; students tune out this daily transmission and the teacher then sees them as unmotivated. Schmoker (2007b) suggested that if students are going to develop the intellectual capacity to read and utilize the essence of the message in textual material, they must be active seekers of information who use reading as a tool in the quest for knowledge. This is a dramatic departure from the transmission model, where the teacher tells students information. Instead of using listening as the predominant way of learning, students can become the seekers of information rather than simply the receivers of information. Seekers of information are more likely to be interested and motivated to learn new things. Guthrie and Wigfield (2000) found that level of student engagement was one of the most important factors to affect outcomes in reading. Their research showed that a base for motivation and engagement was formed by engaging students in literacy events, providing opportunities for social interaction, and helping students set goals.

There are many factors that impact whether a learner takes in information and understands it. Not only do motivation and engagement impact learning in individuals, learners must also bring with them their knowledge of language, that particular content, and their background experiences. Additionally, the context in which the learning takes place—including the social interactions between students, the classroom norms, and the classroom environment—can impact learning. How material is presented—through written text, visually, or orally—has an impact on the learning that takes place as well. Figure 1.1 outlines these factors that teachers need to think about as they plan lessons and engage students in learning activities.

Research in Literacy

What does research say about the literacy practices that help adolescents learn? Students learn through a variety of contexts in secondary schools, including texts, teacher direct instruction, and past and evolving media. They need a reliable and structured process to be able to navigate through the variety of resources in order to gather, remember, and understand information. Research shows that an understanding of how information is structured, connected, and presented is critical to comprehending the intended meaning of the information (Simonsen, 1996). Whether a student will be reading, listening, or viewing information, the student needs to follow a process to understand the structure, connections, and presentation of a set of information.

Being able to understand what they are reading, hearing, or viewing at the secondary level requires that students have sophisticated comprehension abilities that require continuing instruction. There

Figure 1.1 Factors That Impact Learning

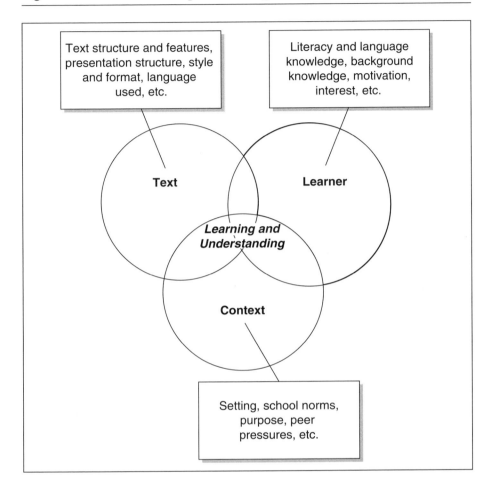

are several important areas of instruction that have been shown to be effective in working with adolescents in the content areas. One of the most frequently mentioned areas is that of developing comprehension strategies (Alvermann, 2001; Biancarosa & Snow, 2004; Moore et al., 1999; Tovani, 2004). Comprehension strategies that students need to learn include using their background knowledge, asking questions, determining the important ideas, monitoring and fixing up thinking when things aren't making sense, creating sensory images—both in-the-head as well as in graphic representations—and synthesizing. Each of these can be taught through explicit instruction with opportunities for the teacher to do think-aloud modeling of the processes she or he is using.

Using background knowledge on a specific topic for comprehension, thinking, and understanding is crucial to the higher-level thinking adolescents need to do (Willingham, 2006). Background knowledge provides a structure for thinking. Using the analogy of a closet, people need hangers in their closets in order to better find clothes and even to think about the clothes they have. In their brains, they need hangers to categorize and use new information. For example, to truly understand the civil rights movement in the United States, students have to have a clear, in-depth understanding of slavery and its underpinnings—the hangers in the closet. This background knowledge allows them to think more critically about how and why the civil rights movement got started and why there was so much resistance to the idea of integration. In addition, background knowledge provides a base for thinking when text becomes difficult. Background knowledge gives the reader something to stand on while they access new information.

Learners should be actively engaged readers. Actively engaged readers ask themselves questions before they read, while they are reading, and after they read. They wonder about things and hypothesize about the author's meaning, intent, and style (Keene & Zimmerman, 2007). Readers may also ask themselves questions to help remember new information. For example, a reader might turn textbook headings into questions and then read to find the answers as a way to remember the important points of that section of the text. At times, readers may have questions that are not directly stated in the text and may continue reading to find possible answers to their questions or move to other resources to find answers. Often, experienced readers don't realize that they are asking questions as they read. That is why it is important to make visible to students how to ask good questions and how to train their mind to attend to the questions they are asking.

Being able to determine what is important is critical when learning new information—whether from texts, lectures, or other media. Oftentimes, in order to engage the learner, authors and speakers will add interesting facts to their books and lectures. For example, in Jean Fritz's (1997) book *Shh! We're Writing the Constitution*, she included interesting facts, such as that George Washington had wooden false teeth and that Ben Franklin was carried to the Constitutional Convention in a chair held above the muddy streets. The section of the book that includes these interesting details also tells about the grievances of the colonists and the events that led up to the convention. In several classes, students remembered the interesting facts but not the overall importance of why the colonists began their journey to freedom from Britain—the more important idea to remember. Determining what is important is also critical when listening and taking lecture notes. Even when listening, knowing which points are important or critical to understanding is necessary as they must be sorted from lecturers' asides and stories.

Summarizing, another important comprehension strategy, builds directly on being able to determine what is important. In order to summarize, a person must take the relevant information and pull it together in a cohesive way. Using the Jean Fritz book example, a summary of information about the Constitutional Convention would not include information about Washington's teeth. In the same way, a summary of a lecture would include only the salient points.

Proficient learners monitor their understanding. They know when they lose track of the meaning and take action to get it back. If reading, they might reread to gain understanding or discuss the difficult section with others. They might also use their background knowledge, or go to other sources to gain background knowledge, before tackling the difficult part again. Often, adolescent readers give up when a text becomes difficult. That is why it is important to explicitly teach several actions students can take to assist with comprehension (Keene & Zimmerman, 2007; Tovani, 2000). Several of these fix-up actions include changing the pace of the reading: slowing down for tricky parts, stopping to think about what has been read to determine what was important, or thinking about questions. Sometimes it helps to summarize orally or in writing what is known and understood up to that point. This might focus a rereading or point the reader forward. Visualizing or sketching a graphic organizer can help refocus a reader as well. These fix-up strategies can be explicitly taught and are useful before, during, or after reading.

While forming sensory images is useful as a fix-up strategy, it is also useful in helping learners develop deeper insights into what they are reading. Thinking about feelings, smells, and sounds can bring something to life—whether it is science, social studies, or any other content area. Tovani (2004) uses an example of a description of smallpox's effect on people from a book used in a science classroom, where the students were asked to draw pictures of the effects they read about. They could have been asked to write about the sounds they may have heard in the hospitals filled with victims of smallpox, or they might have been asked to talk about the emotions of the scientists and doctors working to cure the disease. Bringing sensory images into play deepens understanding.

Another form of visualizing that is helpful in deepening understanding is graphic representation of information and information relationships. Graphic organizers can take many forms, such as KWL

(Know, Want to know, Learned; Ogle, 1986), comparison charts, chains (for chronological listings), webs (for description and relationships), and so on. Being able to take information and see how it can be organized in different ways using a visual representation helps readers connect and categorize information in ways that are meaningful.

Being able to synthesize information is a high-level strategy. Synthesizing means going beyond summarizing what has been read or learned to come up with new ways of thinking that build on past understandings and newly learned information. Synthesis requires the learner to take a variety of ideas from different sources of information and their background knowledge to come up with newly constructed knowledge. It includes understanding theme, revising opinions, adding to something they already know, understanding a different perspective, or coming up with an original idea (Harvey & Goudvis, 2007).

In addition to comprehension strategies, learners need to understand the terminology of the different content areas as well as the general vocabulary often used in academic settings. Vocabulary development is a critical part of content literacy. However, vocabulary is more than listing words with definitions for students to study before a reading, a video, or a lecture. For vocabulary development to make a difference, students must be actively engaged in using the words in a variety of ways. They also need to discuss the nuances and shades of word meanings to understand how a word is used in a particular context and why that specific word was chosen. Showing the connections of words to other words through semantic organizers allows for greater access to precise meaning. Understanding vocabulary has a direct effect on comprehension.

When learners are reading to gain content knowledge, understanding how expository texts are structured and how they may be structured in various content areas is important for understanding. There are basic patterns of expository text that include sequence, description, comparison, and cause and effect. Understanding these structures—what they look like and what key words signal the structure—can aid in understanding. Using the knowledge of text structure to construct mental maps or graphic organizers provides organization for information. For example, knowing that a text section is structured as a comparison/contrast allows the reader to mentally or graphically organize what they are reading in that way.

It is important to remember that texts are tools for learning, and simply reading a textbook will not provide for the depth of understanding in content areas that secondary students need. Having a variety of texts written from a variety of perspectives allows for the synthesis of knowledge. This also allows for thinking that goes beyond simple recall of information. In addition, there are many resources available today for gaining information. Using electronic media and understanding how it is structured is also important—whether text-based, oral, or visual in nature.

How This Book Helps

In this chapter, we outlined both the issues surrounding adolescent literacy today and some important areas for developing literacy and content knowledge. In the rest of this book, we will provide a framework for an instructional process that focuses on before, during, and after reading activities that include a variety of whole-group, small-group, and individual activities to engage students in their own learning. The instructional practices within the structured plan can lead students not only to be better readers, writers, and learners, but also to have greater mastery over the content being taught. We hope that our combined understandings—through Dan's expertise in instructional knowledge at the secondary level and Sarah's knowledge of literacy processes—will provide a base for helping secondary students to learn.

We also hope that by using the processes outlined in this book, teachers will find useful methods for facilitating both student learning and engagement in literacy and in the content areas. The process follows the basic concepts found in much of the literature about successful literacy development and is in a format that takes teacher time into consideration. In these processes, students are engaged in prereading, during-reading, and postreading activities. We are using the term *reading* broadly here to include not only reading but also listening to a lecture, watching a video, or engaging in any other types of learning activities in the classroom. Students should be engaged in the before-, during-, and after-learning process even if other means of accessing information beyond reading are used. In this book, we will focus on reading in particular; however, many of the examples could be useful when instruction includes listening, viewing, or multimedia learning.

2

The Instructional Process

In this chapter, we provide an overview of a basic instructional framework that secondary teachers can use to increase student learning in the subject area being taught while improving reading ability at the same time. The following chapters provide greater detail for each part of the instructional framework as well as many sample lesson plans. The samples are from different middle school, high school, and vocational school subject areas, and they provide a clear process for improving content learning and literacy practices. Our intention is for the instructional practices in this book to be simple and effective models that teachers can use and adapt for their own teaching situation.

We have organized this instructional framework into a series of steps before, during, and after reading assignments—a common organization for effective reading instruction. This framework provides opportunities both for in-the-moment assessment for teacher decision making and for the active involvement of students throughout the content-area lesson. For example, before asking students to read, a teacher may ask students what they already know about the topic, as in the *know* part of a KWL (Know, Want to know, Learned; Ogle, 1986) activity. If the entire class is adding ideas to a chart, everyone gains access to the knowledge that others have while the teacher can see gaps in the background knowledge students bring.

During reading, students may be asked to write down questions they have as they read. The teacher can then circulate around the room to see what questions students have—an assessment while the students are actively thinking about their reading—and monitor their understanding of the material. After reading and some discussion or small-group work, the teacher may ask for exit slips as students leave the classroom. On the exit slips, students list what they have learned that day or are asked either to write down something they didn't understand or to write down their questions. Teachers then have a quick assessment that can guide their planning for whether to reteach the lesson or continue on. Students are again actively engaged in thinking about the material they read and their own learning. It is critical that those activities provide for the active involvement of students in the content information while at the same time improving reading ability.

The lessons shown in Figures 2.1 and 2.2, an English lesson on the analysis and evaluation of editorials by Robin Callahan and an earth science lesson by Chris Neff, illustrate the instructional framework.

Figure 2.1   Lesson on Editorial Analysis

LESSON ON EDITORIAL ANALYSIS AND EVALUATION

Teacher Introductory Statement: Students will analyze the editorial writers' use of fact and opinion to convey their positions on given issues. Students will evaluate which writer creates the *most* compelling argument based on the editorial's strengths and weaknesses—rather than whether or not they agree with the writer's position.

This lesson may span a series of two to three days. Throughout this lesson, when students are working in groups or working independently, the teacher circulates around the classroom serving as a facilitator.

Prereading

Step 1: The teacher will ask students to work in a group of three to generate a list of controversial issues (local, national, or international).

Step 2: The teacher will ask for volunteers to write these issues on the board. The class will select at least three issues and delve into the factors that create the controversy.

Step 3: The teacher will then ask the students to add to their brainstorming by thinking of at least three different ways people can express their opinions on an issue (Web site, blog, debate, editorial . . .). The teachers and students will discuss the benefits and limitations of each medium.

Step 4: Students will then be asked to find at least two editorials on the same issue that demonstrate opposing viewpoints.

Students can choose their articles from newspapers, Newsbank, or online papers such as *USA Today's* Opposing Views (blogs.usatoday.com/oped)

Variation: The teacher can start by selecting two model editorials with opposing viewpoints so that the students can receive feedback from their peers and observe the teacher modeling these thinking strategies.

During Reading

Students will complete the Editorial Analysis Reading Guide for each editorial. By following these precise directions, students will transact with the text, and be actively engaged in the reading and writing process, thereby improving their comprehension.

Step 1: Students will annotate the text by doing the following:

- Highlighting the facts in one color
- Highlighting the writer's opinion in another color
- Writing marginal notes (questions, reactions, connections . . .)

Note: If students are working on the same editorials, they can compare their highlighting and transactions. By discussing their similarities and differences, they can refine their understanding of fact and opinion as well as the fundamental components of argumentation. The color coding engages the visual and kinesthetic learners.

Step 2: Students will complete the questions on the Editorial Analysis Reading Guide. These items are designed to take the students through each of the levels of Bloom's taxonomy and to extend their connections beyond the text. They will use these answers as the basis for their postreading assignment. The teacher will collect these responses and evaluate them prior to the postreading assignment.

Postreading

Step 1: Students will review the teacher's feedback and ask for clarification.

Step 2: Students will write an essay in response to the following prompt:

- Which of the two editorials presents the *most effective* argument on this controversial issue? Use at least two specific examples (quotes) from the selection to support your choice.

Step 3: Students will share their essays with a group of three. They will evaluate one another's reasoning and discuss how these editorials affected their view of the controversial topic.

Step 4: The teacher will then lead the class in a group discussion to debrief the strategies and skills they have gained.

(Continued)

Figure 2.1 (Continued)

Name: _____

Teacher: Mrs. Callahan

EDITORIAL ANALYSIS READING GUIDE

Directions:

a. Read through the entire editorial once to discover the main idea.

b. Read the editorial a second time. Annotate the text.
  - Highlight the facts in one color
  - Highlight the writer's opinions in another color
  - Write marginal notes (questions, reactions, connections . . .)

c. Answer the questions in **complete sentences.**

d. Support your observations with **quotes from the article.**

e. Attach the editorial to the top of this analysis when you are finished.

Title: _____

Writer: _____

1. What is the main topic (major argument)?

2. Summarize the major ideas in the editorial.

3. Facts: What are two key facts (record the exact quotes)? Why are these facts important to the writer's argument?

   a.

   Importance:

   b.

   Importance:

4. Opinions: What are two key opinions (record the exact quotes)? Do you agree or disagree with this opinion? Why or why not?

   a.

   Your reaction:

   b.

   Your reaction:

5. Evaluation:

   a. What strengths did the writer demonstrate in this editorial (purpose, logic, balance . . .)?

   b. What are the weaknesses (fallacies, tone . . .)? What could the writer have done to improve this argument?

   c. Has your opinion changed about this issue? Why or why not?

6. Write two questions that you have about this issue that would *require further research*?

   a.

   b.

Source: Developed by Mrs. Robin Lynn Callahan, English teacher and reading specialist.

Robin began her lesson with students brainstorming current controversial issues and how people might express their opinions on those issues. She then asked students to go and search for their own editorials to read. As you can see from the lesson plan, Robin also included a variation of the lesson that provided modeling before students did their own investigations as a way to offer more support for students. Since different classes have different students, teachers need to adapt plans to meet the needs of the particular students in their class. Her before-reading activity set the stage for finding appropriate readings.

Figure 2.2   Earth Science Lesson

LESSON ON EARTH SCIENCE: THREE TYPES OF ROCKS

Teacher Introductory Statement: By the time that we are finished with class today, you will know that there are three types of rocks on earth: sedimentary, metamorphic, and igneous. You will be able to name the three types and tell the class something about each type.

Prereading

Step 1: The teacher will move to each group of desks and place a bucket filled with rocks in the middle of the group of students. As the teacher is doing this, he or she will tell students what they will be learning.

Step 2: The teacher will give the students approximately ninety seconds to dump the rocks on the desks and begin to look at the rocks and feel the rocks. The teacher will tell them to touch them and look at them in an attempt to identify differences.

Step 3: The teacher will tell students that they have three minutes to separate the rocks into three piles and to attempt to place rocks together that feel alike, look alike, or have some distinguishing characteristics that make them similar to other rocks in that pile.

Step 4: The students will work together to separate the rocks into three distinct piles.

Step 5: While students are separating the rocks, the teacher will give each group of students a sheet of paper with three columns, like the one below.

Group 1	Group 2	Group 3
1.		
2.		
3.		

Step 6: The teacher will request that each group report what they have done, with one reporter from each group telling the class about their groupings.

Step 7: Then, the teacher will tell students to scan the pages in a textbook chapter on types of rocks.

Step 8: When students finish the scan, the teacher will ask, "What did you notice?" Students will offer responses about information on rocks.

Step 9: The teacher will tell students that within this chapter, they will find information that will tell them what type of rock to write in the blank space at the bottom of the sheets where they wrote the characteristics of each pile of rocks.

During Reading

Step 1: The teacher will assign the reading of specific pages in the chapter. The pages that the teacher tells them to move to are the pages that offer descriptions of the three types of rocks: sedimentary, metamorphic, and igneous.

Step 2: The teacher will tell the students to be sure to read those pages that include a chart and pictures of the different kinds of rocks.

Step 3: The students will keep the charts they made while separating rocks on their desks beside their books as they read.

Step 4: The teacher will tell the students that when they read a description of a rock that is the same as a description that they wrote on their original chart, they should place a checkmark beside the trait on their chart.

Step 5: The teacher tells students that when they are finished reading, they should have checked off most of the descriptions that they placed on their charts.

Step 6: The teacher gives students about ten minutes to read the three pages and check their charts.

Step 7: The teacher asks the students to stop reading and checking. The teacher then directs them to return to their small-group situation.

Postreading

Step 1: The teacher tells the students to review the lists they made while they were making the three piles of rocks. Their goal is to identify each of the piles of rocks that they had categorized on their three-column list.

Step 2: The teacher tells students that as a group, they will decide which pile contains which type of rocks. As a group they must decide between sedimentary, metamorphic, and igneous and list one of the three under each of the lists that they made initially.

Step 3: The teacher tells each group that they will pick one person to report to the whole class about how and why they identified each of their piles of rocks the way they did.

Step 4: One student from each group will make an oral report to the class on their learning about the types of rocks and their characteristics.

Source: Developed by Mr. Chris Neff, science teacher.

In contrast, Chris began his lesson by arousing curiosity and having students begin to think about the characteristics of rocks before they read about them. This before-reading activity engaged students in thinking about rocks and beginning to form categories or structures for thinking about the reading to come.

In the English example, during the reading of the different editorials, students were engaged in highlighting and taking marginal notes. Since Robin asked students to use one highlighter color for facts and a different color for opinions, she could easily see if individual students had difficulty understanding the concepts of fact and opinion as she walked around the room. This provided her with an on-the-spot assessment of the basics of the lesson and an opportunity to confer with students to clear up any misunderstandings. Students also had an opportunity to talk with others when reading the same editorials for comparison and discussion of the facts and opinions presented. Robin also provided an "Editorial Analysis Reading Guide." This provided a frame for thinking during the reading and also a quick assessment as she collected and analyzed the guides before she gave an after-reading assignment.

In the science lesson, the during-reading activity engaged students in matching their own categorization system and the characteristics they developed in the small groups with the information they were reading. As soon as they noticed something in the reading that corresponded to their own thinking from the prereading activity, they noted that right away. This provided an active way to confirm their thinking while reading.

In the English lesson, after the reading of the editorials and the written work during the reading, Robin gave students an opportunity to discuss the notes they had made on their guides. She then gave them feedback on their notes and asked them to write essays about the effectiveness of the editorials and the impact they had on their views of the controversial issue. Students had the opportunity to be actively engaged in discussing their essays and what they learned with each other in small groups. Robin finished the lesson with a discussion of what they learned about the reading and writing skills and strategies involved in the lesson.

After the reading assignment in the science lesson, the small groups met again to discuss and refine their thinking and prepare a presentation that one member of the group would present to the entire class. Through developing an oral report, the small-group members had to think about the important points from the readings on identifying rocks and tie them to the actual rocks they had analyzed.

These examples show how lessons can be planned while keeping in mind improved student learning and engagement in literacy and in the content areas. They are only two examples that illustrate ways to engage students in content learning and reading improvement.

Before-Reading Activities

As can be seen in the previous examples, the basic purpose of before-reading activities is to activate or develop background knowledge, to establish purpose and relevancy, and/or to build curiosity. Prereading activities may also allow the teacher to assess the background knowledge of students and their understanding of any content-specific vocabulary they may encounter.

There are many different activities designed to prepare students for reading. Some are designed for use by individuals, such as writing to a quote from the material to be read, reading questions at the end of a chapter before reading, or giving quizzes in anticipation of the reading passage. Prereading activities may also provide opportunities for small-group discussions about illustrations and author purpose or for brainstorming background knowledge based on headings.

Predicting is another prereading strategy that students can use. In a textbook, students can write down or discuss predictions about what will happen in sections of a text based on the headings. Students can also predict word meanings by reading a small section of the text that includes a target vocabulary word and extrapolating from usage what it might mean in this particular reading. In addition, predictions can be made about readings based on illustrations, table of contents, or through the use of background knowledge on the subject.

During-Reading Activities

In the English example, the during-reading activities provided the teacher with opportunities for quick assessment and individualized teaching and provided students with a focus for their reading. The earth science example provided students with an opportunity to use the information from the reading while they were in the process of reading.

There are a variety of activities that can engage student thinking during reading. During-reading activities can help students better understand what they are reading, remember the information from the text, and improve how they think as a reader during the reading process. For example, the teacher may provide questions that are answered during reading or ask students to generate their own questions while reading. Students might also use sticky notes during reading to mark tricky vocabulary or places in the text they weren't sure they understood. Sticky notes might also be used to mark important points or points that students would like to discuss. Also, graphic organizers may be provided for students to complete while reading to keep them actively organizing the new information.

After-Reading Activities

In Robin's example, the after-reading activity included student essays that demonstrated their learning on evaluating editorials. Writing can be an important after-reading activity. Writing slows down thought processes and allows for categorizing and structuring thoughts. It provides links to background knowledge and to the organization of thoughts and experiences in a way that cannot be done through talking about a text or just reading it. Asking children to respond to reading through writing also develops the ability to more thoughtfully synthesize the information they have read (Mahurt, 2005).

Exit slips are a form of quick writing at the end of a period that can be used to assess understanding while also helping students synthesize their thoughts. Exit slips can include a specific question or students can develop their own questions around important ideas or questions they still have about the material. Exit slips can also be open-ended responses to the day's learning.

After the science experience and reading, students developed and made oral presentations on what they had learned. In addition to writing and presenting, students can complete graphic organizers, make PowerPoint lessons for future classes, or illustrate or sketch what they have learned.

The Process

By engaging students in activities before, during, and after reading, students are provided both with support for learning content knowledge and with a model for approaching texts. In addition to content knowledge, students learn strategies that will help them with anything they read. In this way, the lesson activities and procedures become more than just something that is done during a specific class. The activities lead students to actions they can take whenever they are reading anything in any class.

For students to make this connection between the in-class activities and their own reading, teachers need to make the literacy-learning piece of instruction explicit by clearly stating what students are learning that can help them as readers. For example, as part of prereading activities, a teacher may ask students in the class to preview the text. In addition to the content objective of activating background knowledge on the concepts to be introduced in the reading, teachers can also make statements such as the following: *Readers preview text sections before they read and think about what they already know about the topic. This is something you can do before any reading assignment.* Explicit statements help students who are not connecting classroom work with their own reading to hear a clear message on how to use the specific activity in a more general way.

Another example of explicit language from prereading could come from a teacher who has engaged the class in developing questions about what they will be reading. The teacher could make a clear statement, such as, *Today we developed a set of questions before we read. Readers do that all the time. Whenever you are preparing to read, think about some questions you might have on that topic.* If students have been asked to look specifically at text structure before reading, another statement might be, *Readers think about how a book is organized and how that structure might help them think about the information they are reading. You can do that with any book you are going to read.*

Teachers can also make explicit statements about reading processes as part of during and after activities. For example, if a questioning activity was used during in-class reading, the teacher could restate the content objectives and also make a clear statement about reading process, such as, *Readers ask themselves questions as they read. They wonder about things and read on to find answers. This is something you can do whenever you read.* If summary writing was done after reading, explicit statements after that activity could be, *Readers summarize what they read to remember important facts. Writing a summary can help you remember what you have read. You can do this whenever you read and want to remember vital information.* If small-group discussion was used after reading, teachers might say, *Readers talk to others about what they have read to better understand the content of that reading. You can do that with your friends after you read anything.*

Some students make the connections between class activities and use the strategies from class in other situations, while other students need overt statements before they make those connections. These explicit statements help all students see that activities in one content classroom can facilitate their reading in any subject area where reading is assigned, or even when reading for purposes outside of school. These types of explicit statements make it clear to students that they can use what they have been doing as part of a particular class assignment and apply it whenever they engage in reading.

We are advocating in this book that teachers provide opportunities for students to engage in activities before, during, and after reading in order to improve students' abilities to understand content knowledge and to improve reading comprehension. It is important for students to be actively engaged in their own reading process for more effective learning and even more effectively managed classrooms, while at the same time working within the typical time constraints of secondary schools. In the following chapters, we provide more details and sample lessons to show how lessons can be developed following the before, during, and after framework in a step-by-step method that teachers will find easy to adapt for their own classrooms.

3

Before Reading

We met with Michelle Bonser after she had completed a session with students struggling in mathematics. Michelle is a mathematics support teacher in a high school that is focused on helping all students who have difficulty with understanding algebra concepts. Michelle told us that most of her students have challenges because they do not pay attention to detail or they have difficulty with reading. One of her strategies for improving math achievement is to start all students with a prelearning model that does not include any numbers. She contends that if students do not learn how to use words in the context of mathematics, they will be confused with the problem-solving process.

When we watched one of her classes, we didn't see numbers or formulas. Instead, students were working on logic puzzles that were all textually based. For example, the students read a series of eight sentences and then completed a table that identified names of students and their corresponding characteristics. In order to complete the table, the students had to carefully read all eight sentences to find information that attached itself to a particular name. Some of the individual descriptors were not literally present in the eight sentences, but through analysis of information and use of the table facts, the students could infer the names of individuals, the year the individuals would graduate from high school, a person's favorite sport, and the profession that each person planned to enter.

As we observed the exercise, we recognized that Michelle was preparing students to think and to anticipate specific information within mathematics texts. She was, in effect, facilitating a practice session on the skills needed to do the lesson. She did this before the students went into the math text to read or start doing the numbers and formulas necessary to complete math problems for that day.

When we went to the next room in the very same school, we saw Jack Moyer using prereading as a condition of solving math word problems. Jack assigned students five word problems to be completed within a set time during the class. On each student's desk was a page filled with graphic organizers that required students to break out the information found within a problem before the students started to work on the problems themselves.

Jack told us that most students rush into math problems without thinking about them. He also thinks that students do not do enough reading, processing, and planning prior to attempting to solve problems. Because of this, he required students to skim the word problems and look for words and information prior to actually reading any of the problems in depth and before attempting to solve them (see Table 3.1). He also wanted students to talk to each other before they worked on

Table 3.1   Math Prereading Activity

Step 1	Scan through the question.	
Step 2	What words do you see that you do not know?	Words that I do not know are:
Step 3	If there are words that you do not know, talk with a classmate about what the word means or is. (If your classmate cannot help you, both of you should come to Mr. Moyer.)	What do my words mean?
Step 4	Read the math problem slowly.	
Step 5	What do you believe the problem is asking you to do?	I think that the problem is asking me to:
Step 6	Talk to a classmate about what you think the problem is asking you to do.	My classmate and I think that this word problem wants us to:

problems. He contends that without this prereading activity, students have difficulty solving problems because they have not planned how to solve them.

Research has indicated that it is vitally important for learners to activate and use what they already know prior to beginning a learning or reading act (Anderson, Spiro, & Anderson, 1978; Strangman & Hall, 2004). Learners need to think and become actively engaged in preparing mind structures for the new information they will be receiving through text, teacher instruction, or different media. Having a plan for current and possible learning gives the learner a cognitive structure for retaining, organizing, and thinking deeply about the new information. Since study in content areas requires the retention of information, it is critical that students have an information network for retaining information. Remembering information on a topic where no background knowledge exists is difficult because there are no existing networks in the mind on which the new information can be hooked (Willingham, 2006). Once learners have some knowledge, they can build on what they know by making links from what they know to the new information; they develop new associations between the old and new information. These connections aid in remembering, and this is particularly important for reading comprehension.

In this chapter, we will provide an instructional process for teachers to use to help students actively engage in their own prereading—keeping in mind the importance of active student engagement. These instructional processes facilitate students' understanding of the content being learned as well as develop their ability to comprehend future learning experiences. The goal is to provide students with strategies for thinking about and organizing information that will help them learn that particular content as well as help them learn how to learn. We will also focus on several areas of before-reading instructional practices that guide students in their learning and provide them with strategies they can use in the future when working independently. We discuss the assessment, development, and activation of student background knowledge as well as forms of questioning that can guide student learning. Using text structure for better comprehension as an important aspect of prereading is discussed along with vocabulary development.

Some of the prereading instructional strategies to be introduced are student- and teacher-developed questions; know, want to know, and learned (KWL) charts (Ogle, 1986); anticipation guides (Readance, Bean, & Baldwin, 1998); and direct instruction in needed knowledge. All of these instructional activities have the goal of helping students to develop and activate relevant background knowledge for the reading and learning to come.

It is important to keep in mind that the goal is not for students to become dependent on the teacher's activities to provide or activate background knowledge, but rather for students to learn how to activate the knowledge they bring to any reading or learning situation and to learn ways to gain knowledge if they don't feel they have sufficient background. The goal is to explicitly teach students habits of thinking and to guide their use of such practices with the idea of moving toward independent use. This means that teachers will gradually release responsibility for taking strategic action to students so that

> the application of new knowledge progresses from explicit instruction with high teacher support to independent application with no teacher support. Instruction moves from activities that require modeling of a strategic activity, to engaging learners through shared and guided practice, to finally involving learners in opportunities for independent application. (Mahurt, Metcalfe, & Gwyther, 2007, p. 3)

Background Knowledge

An initial step in this process is for the teacher to explicitly state what students are expected to learn from the lesson. A concise statement to orient students to the new learning is all that is needed. Some teachers write the purpose for the lesson on the board. Students then see it when they walk into the room. For example, in a class on travel and tourism, the teacher, Donna Harris, stated, "By the end of this lesson, you will be able to explain the importance of the menu, list basic categories of menus, describe fixed-menu schedules, and describe cycle-menu schedules." This step—stating expected learning—prepares student thinking for the next step in prereading: developing or activating background knowledge.

Background knowledge or prior knowledge is defined as *all the knowledge a person brings to the reading act*. It includes concept knowledge, knowledge of the world, and an understanding of reading and writing processes (Strangman & Hall, 2004). Since students bring a wide range of knowledge to reading and learning, it is important that they not only use that knowledge but also be able to reliably determine what prior knowledge is relevant for a particular learning situation (Duke, 2006). For example, when preparing to read a section of a high school biology textbook on DNA, students may know about the use of DNA to identify people in criminal or missing persons investigations. However, as they preview the chapter, they may note how the book is structured and realize that the headings or sections of text do not reflect what they currently know about the topic. They may see that most sections provide them with new and expanded information. Then, as they read, they may be integrating what they already know about the use of DNA with the new and more detailed information from the textbook.

Because background knowledge is so critical (Willingham, 2006), one thing that teachers need to do before planning a lesson is determine whether students have the necessary background knowledge to read the textbook being used in the class or if they have the background knowledge to understand lecture information or information from other media. Some teachers worry that by providing background knowledge before a lesson they are not allowing students to use their reading or listening skills—which they assume students in secondary schools already know how to do. However, textbooks are complex and often densely constructed, with a great deal of information on each page. Since it is the role of the teacher to guide student learning, it makes sense that they may need guidance in textbook reading as well. As Readance, Bean, and Baldwin (1998) pointed out, if textbooks were meant for students to read without any assistance, students would simply learn through reading and teachers wouldn't be needed for further explanations. In addition, a teacher lecturing to impart the same information that is in the text does not encourage student reading or the development of a reading base in that particular content area. What is needed is the idea that "every teacher teaches students to learn with texts" (Readance, Bean, & Baldwin, 1998, p. 6); it provides a foundation for the importance of guiding secondary students to develop and activate background knowledge before reading.

Developing Questions

Teachers need to make decisions about whether students have enough background knowledge to engage in a learning situation or a text reading and then decide how to build that knowledge if they feel students do not have the depth of knowledge they need. If teachers determine that students have the background they need, then the decision about how to activate that knowledge needs to be made. There are several different ways that teachers can assess and activate the background knowledge of students before they read.

One way to assess as well as activate background knowledge is to have all students in the class brainstorm all they know about a topic (Daniels & Zemelman, 2004). In this way, all the students in the class are exposed to the knowledge that others in the class have. While this can be helpful in gauging the knowledge of the class and stimulating everyone's thinking, it doesn't allow the teacher to find out what individuals know or uncover any individual misconceptions that need to be cleared up.

Another way to assess and activate background knowledge is to ask specific, structured questions (McKenna & Robinson, 1997). The teacher may ask a set of questions, beginning with easier ones and continuing on to more difficult questions as correct answers are given. Another form of questioning is for teachers to prepare questions that require written responses. These may be open-ended, specific, or even multiple choice questions. For example, in an electronics class on capacitance, Robert Marino, the teacher, asked students to complete the anticipation guide in Figure 3.1 with a partner as a way to both activate prior knowledge and to find out what students already knew about the topic. In this example, the anticipation quiz prepared students for what they were going to learn by providing explicit information about learning expectations and also gave the teacher information for further teaching.

Anticipation guides may also be used in a true/false or agree/ disagree format to gauge student understanding and to get them

Figure 3.1   Electronics Class Anticipation Quiz

1. The _____ of a capacitor is an insulator.

2. The base unit of capacitance is the _____.

3. The capacitor current _____ as the capacitor voltage increases.

4. When charged, the capacitor voltage equals the _____ voltage.

5. Charging current is controlled by the value of _____ and the current capacity of the source.

thinking about what they know. In a physics class on linear momentum and impulse, Steve Shadel, the teacher, wanted to focus on the terms *momentum* and *impulse* by tying those physics concepts to agree/disagree statements in an anticipation/reaction guide (see Table 3.2). After completing the anticipation/reaction guide individually, and before reading the selection, students were asked to work in small groups to develop questions that came to mind while they were completing the anticipation guide. Steve collected the guides and quickly looked them over while the students were in their small groups to assess the background knowledge that individual students had. In addition to guiding the students to think and question before reading, the guides also gave Steve an idea of what he might need to talk about before asking the students to begin reading independently. He was able to determine what the students already knew in order to guide their reading.

Another form of assessing and activating prior knowledge is to ask students to develop their own questions about a topic. This is the second step in the KWL process (Ogle, 1986), where students think about and chart things they know about a topic and then develop

Table 3.2   Anticipation/Reaction Guide

Directions: Before reading references and answering questions on the Web, **check** the before-reading statements with agree or disagree.

Anticipation Guide Before Reading		
Agree	*Disagree*	*Momentum and Impulse*
		Force is **the only thing** that must be known to determine the change in momentum of an object.
		Momentum is also known as *mass in motion*.
		If it takes an impulse of 13,000 N·sec to stop a car going 80 km/hr, it will take an impulse of 26,000 N·sec to get the same car going at 80 km/hr from a stop.
		Getting shot can really throw you for a loop.
		Momentum is not conserved in *elastic collisions*.
		Momentum is not conserved in *inelastic collisions*.

questions about things they want to learn, as seen in Table 3.3. In Donna Harris's lesson on menu styles and schedules, she asked students to meet in small groups and talk about all the things they had seen on menus. After this discussion, she completed the first two columns of the KWL chart with the class. Donna listed all the things students said they had seen on menus on this chart. Then, she asked each student to write a question he or she had about menus. Students again met with their small groups to discuss their questions and possible answers to their questions and then share the questions they still had to list on the KWL chart.

In this example, involvement in the KWL process gave students the opportunity to think about what they were going to learn and to have a framework for categorizing and remembering the new information. In addition to learning more about menus, the students were also learning that it is important to think about what you already know before you read and form questions that you might want to have answered while reading. There is evidence that when readers have questions prior to reading, they will seek the answer to those questions as they read. In other words, forming prereading questions allows the students to have a specific purpose for the reading or the lecture to come.

Another example of students developing their own questions can be seen in a lesson on battery inspection and testing. Marty Christian, the teacher, gave each student a two-column chart. One column was

Table 3.3   KWL Chart

What We **K**now	What We **W**ant to Know	What We **L**earned

headed with "Questions I Have" and the other column was headed with "My Answers." He then showed a set of slides depicting battery maintenance to the class (see Figure 3.2) and asked each student to write a question that related to each slide. He then grouped students to discuss all their questions and decide on five to include on a chart. Each group had one blank chart with five spaces on each side of the chart. The students were then going to find answers to the questions that they had developed. These questions were focused specifically on the content to be learned. This student-developed questioning activated prior knowledge and allowed for construction of new information by stimulating the students' curiosity.

Figure 3.2   Sample of Picture Slide From Battery Inspection and Testing Lesson

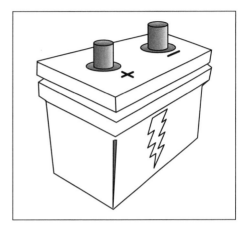

Drawing by Jennifer Taylor.

Understanding and Using Text Structure

Research shows that knowledge of text structure plays an important role in understanding and comprehending texts (Kristo & Bamford, 2004; Smolkin & Donovan, 2002). Understanding how authors have organized their writing provides another set of information that students can use for remembering and organizing new information while reading. Table 3.4 outlines some of the most common structures for informational texts. While no text is structured completely in one way, often sections of texts have an identifiable structure. It is helpful for students to recognize this structure before they read so they can organize their thoughts while they read.

For example, if students preview a section of a textbook with a chapter titled "The Civil War," the students might recognize that one heading under that title was "Root Causes." They would identify that section as most likely a cause and effect organization, so their thinking before they read would be that they need to think about what happened and what caused those things to happen, asking themselves, "What were the reasons for this war? Why did this happen? What events made it happen?" The development of questions based on text structure prior to reading provides a focus for adding the new information while reading and for expanded thinking after reading.

Table 3.4   Structures of Informational Text

Text Structures	Organization	Some Signal Words	Questions That May Come to Mind Before Reading
Description	Describes things in detail. Usually an introduction followed by subtopics.	for example, consists of, looks like, like, another kind	What will this look like? What are the characteristics?
Sequence	Tells the order of steps in a process or a series of events. May be time sequence or in order by steps, numbers, etc.	next, first, last, before, after, another, then, later	What are the steps? What is the timeline of events? In what order did this happen?
Comparison and contrast	Tells about similarities and differences between events or ideas.	like, by, in comparison, although, similar to, different, have in common, but	How are these things going to be alike? Different? How will this compare to what I already know?
Cause and effect	Provides a causal relationship between events—the results and the reasons for those results.	therefore, as a result, for that reason, because	Why did this happen? What are the reasons? What were the results?

Before reading, a teacher could introduce the structure of the reading selection and point out how signal words guide thinking and what signal words might be present in a text that was structured in a particular way. Table 3.4 includes some of the signal words for different text structures. In the cause and effect example, the teacher might ask students to look through the section and find words that signal a reason or cause, such as *therefore, as a result, for that reason, because, so, then,* or *consequently.* By doing this, students can clearly see the structure of the reading and have a cognitive organization prepared for the information they will be reading. Knowing how books are put together can improve comprehension and understanding of text material. Some students have difficulty with "getting lost in the words" (Dymock, 2005, p. 177) and are unable to determine what is important to remember. Knowing the structure of the information being provided can give students a model for thinking and remembering as they learn.

Previewing Text

In addition to talking about text structures and signal words before reading, it is important for students to know how the text is organized and to activate background knowledge by previewing the text itself—a "walk-through" of the reading selection (McKenna & Robinson, 1997). A walk-through orients the reader to the book with teacher guidance, but it is an action that students can take on their own and use as they read and learn independently. If we think of what experienced adult readers do before reading a book—read the back and front cover information, think about the author and what they know about that person, read his or her biographical information if available, and perhaps think about the topic—they are walking through the book and orienting themselves to a new reading. Through the process of previewing, we are teaching students lifelong literacy and learning skills.

When introducing a text to the class for the first time, students should be guided to preview the entire book to see how it is set up, what resources (such as glossaries) are available, and what the appendices offer. Reading the table of contents sets students up for understanding the format for the entire book, while leafing through the book shows how pictures and charts are used in the text. Once students are familiar with the whole text, there will still need to be opportunities for more closely previewing each of the sections that students will read.

Before a specific reading assignment in a content-area classroom, previewing activities should guide students to read chapter titles and headings while looking for key words and possible text structures in different sections. This previewing helps build students' thinking about what they already know. In the example from the capacitance lesson, Robert asked student pairs to sample the text while using the anticipation guide as a way to help them not only think about the content but also to notice the text structure and format of the section of the text they were about to read. Background knowledge was triggered by what the preview of the text showed them.

Previewing can lead students to think about the following questions: How is the information organized and how did the author break down the main section into parts? What are the headings making me think about? What text structures do I see? Do I see words that I am familiar with? What do I already know about this?

Vocabulary

In addition to activities for activating and developing background knowledge, talking about vocabulary before reading or learning is important. Vocabulary in content areas represents concepts that are critical to understanding the subject area. In addition, the vocabulary of a subject is one of the tools that people in those areas use, and someone who did not know that vocabulary would have a hard time being part of that community. Every branch of learning and every career area has words that are unique to it and critical for being a part of that career group or learning group. These words are considered to be the technical vocabulary for that discipline (Readance, Bean, & Baldwin, 1998).

In Robert's field of electronics, words like *voltage, current, capacitor, circuits,* and *AC/DC* all have a specific meaning and stand for significant concepts that people working in that field need to know. Those words are part of the technical vocabulary people need to be knowledgeable in the field of electronics. But words like *current* and *circuit* have very different meanings as the technical vocabulary in other fields of study. In electronics, a circuit is *the route around which electrical current can flow.* However, social scientists might talk about circuit courts or a lecture circuit, while someone in physical education might talk about completing a round of exercises in circuit training. A politician might be said to be going against current thinking, while in science oceanographers might talk about ocean currents. Content area teachers must directly instruct their students in the technical vocabulary for the concepts they are teaching in their discipline.

Before students read a text, view a video, or listen to a lecture, it is helpful for them to hear some of the difficult terms that may come up, especially those words that stand for important concepts. This does not mean handing out a list of words with their definitions or asking students to look up words in the dictionary. It means choosing a few of the most important words and quickly stating the words with a definition that is easy to understand and reflects directly on the immediate content to be learned. It is also important to use the words in several sentences to illustrate the meaning in that content area.

Sometimes, teachers might want to briefly introduce some words that students may have difficulty reading or pronouncing. In Donna's lesson on menus, she simply pointed out and pronounced words that students were going to encounter in their reading: *table d'hote, a la carte, cycle menu, room service, banquet, ethnic menu, theme menu, appetizers, entrée, business balance, aesthetic balance, nutritional balance.* This was the extent of introducing these words before the actual reading of the text. Donna came back to these words after the reading for a more thorough discussion and for groups of students to work together to write definitions in their own words.

In Nate Conroy's social studies lesson, he told the students about four key terms that would be found in the reading. Choosing a few key terms allows students to focus on the most important concepts. Nate decided that he would give a brief written explanation of the four important terms and then asked the students to read to develop a more in-depth understanding of the words. As you can see, these short definitions help students on the road to reading but are not in the detail that would be developed after the reading.

Important vocabulary:

1. Popular sovereignty—The right of citizens of a region to vote on legal provisions for their region.

2. Secession—The formal withdrawal of a state from the Union.

3. Abolition—The movement to outlaw slavery.

4. Nativism—The favoring of native-born people over immigrants.

Nate tied concept understanding to vocabulary and held students responsible for coming up with deeper meanings. Student understandings were discussed and further developed by the teacher after the students read the selection.

Terry Sheaffer, an auto repair teacher, gave students the following vocabulary words in a chart (see Table 3.5): *body hammer, buckles, deformation, gouge, hammer-off-dolly, hammer-on-dolly, shrinking metal, spring-back, stretched metal, tensile strength, work hardening,* and *yield strength.* He gave the students three minutes to scan the section of the book they would be reading and write down the page numbers where they found those words. This gave students an opportunity

Table 3.5   Vocabulary Prelearning

Page Number Where Word Is Found	The Words and Terms	Definition
	body hammer	
	buckles	
	deformation	
	gouge	
	hammer-off-dolly	
	hammer-on-dolly	
	shrinking metal	
	spring-back	
	stretched metal	
	tensile strength	
	work hardening	
	yield strength	

to preview that section of text so they would be better able to focus on those words later when they read and completed the definition section of the chart.

These examples are not the end of vocabulary teaching and learning. Much more work on vocabulary should be done during and after reading. You will see evidence of that in upcoming chapters.

The goal of the prereading activities in secondary classrooms is not just to activate knowledge that students already have and guide their thinking about that particular content, although that is important. Prereading activities can also lead students to begin to think about questions to ask themselves before they read. This allows them to have personal purposes for reading and provides the cognitive structures for adding new learning to current understandings. Some important questions that students may ask themselves before reading include

- What is the main topic of what I am going to read?
- What do I already know about this topic?
- What is my purpose for reading this?
- How is this book organized and how will that help me learn from this text?
- What words would I expect to be part of this topic?

While this chapter focuses on prereading, it is hard to separate instructional activities into prereading only. Prereading activities should be reinforced during learning and followed up after learning. However, prereading is crucial. Teachers must provide students with the opportunity to actively engage in stimulating their prior knowledge so that it can be related to what they will read.

4

During Reading

Nicole Fink was one of the first teachers to go through our training. She seemed to buy into the concept readily and immediately began practicing these strategies with students. When we visited her, we were excited to see what she had done. Her entire lesson was based on strategies to help students learn. We were most impressed with the way that she had students involved in the during-learning process.

Nicole started her lesson with a traditional anticipation guide, but during the reading, she required students to answer guiding questions. Some of these questions included page numbers where the information could be found. We questioned this technique because students could simply go to the specified page and answer the questions without ever fully reading the text. Nicole explained that since she teaches science to special education students, she thinks that the students need direction on how and where to find certain information. She pointed out that she only listed page numbers for questions that led to information that was essential for learning the concept being taught.

Nicole said that many of her students were so fearful of misunderstanding what they were reading that they tried to memorize everything and therefore missed certain important facts. This then led them to have difficulty summarizing what they had learned from the reading. By giving students page numbers to find answers to certain key questions, she believed that they focused on the indispensable information that was important to learn. She pointed out that students read more when they had some guide for their learning activity, whether reading, listening to direct instruction, discussing in class, or watching a video. Each type of instructional practice required directed activity led by the teacher in order for students to learn. She said that by giving them activities that led them to focus on particular concepts, the students had a greater chance of learning key concepts as they read.

In addition to engaging in activities to guide their reading, students need to practice. Reading requires practice. Thinking requires practice. Learning requires practice. In order to maintain a skill, there needs to be continual usage of that skill. Simply put, one of the most effective ways to practice these three skills is to read. Reading requires physical and mental skills that must be applied on a regular basis if one is to be strong at comprehending. In order to read successfully, a person must think while reading to connect to and learn from the ideas that are presented in the text. Through reading, students can learn and develop new ideas that can then be used to extend the intellect and knowledge. However, we have discovered from teachers that many high school students do not read. Teachers tell us that students either cannot read or refuse to read when assigned reading. We have even had teachers tell us that they do not assign reading at all because the "kids just won't do it."

Obviously, in these days of accountability and high-stakes testing, this is very disconcerting. As teachers and schools grapple with the issue of whether students can read well enough to demonstrate that they are learning, we recognize that students must practice literacy skills in order to become better readers and learners. Schools spend time and money attempting to find the silver bullet that will increase reading scores, and the problem may not be the technical side of reading as much as it may be the lack of student practice. As one science teacher in one of our workshops stated, "We can fix reading scores by being sure that kids read." Richard Allington (2001) advocated for this idea when he pointed out that by replacing whatever activities go on in classrooms with reading activity, there will be an increase in test scores.

As simple as this may seem, the instructional strategies in this text are based on the assertion that, if secondary schools want students to read better, students must have more opportunities to delve deeply into written discourse. By delving into written material, students are practicing the reading, thinking, and learning skills that lead to reading comprehension. Schmoker (2007a) stated that schools must provide "far more in-class opportunities to read interesting and provocative texts purposefully" (p. 492). He contends that students will not acquire analytical thinking skills until they are required to search through texts that stimulate them to create personal ideas about the material.

Searching through text material and reading it more deeply is what must be the focus of the during-reading experience. The instructional strategies in this chapter provide students with activities that send them into the depths of written material. They also require students to do activities that move beyond just reading words. We believe that when teachers assign reading without requiring engaging activities, students may read without purpose and without solid concentration on the message of the words. In other words, readers could comply with the assignment by reading the words but fail to comprehend what those words really mean.

During prereading, students should engage in activities that help to stimulate prior knowledge. Prior knowledge is necessary so that students can draw connections from what they know to what they are learning. By having already-retained knowledge stimulated, the students have a cognitive structure for the new information. This stimulation must not stop with prereading if strong comprehension is going to occur. Students must actively engage with the text for what they are supposed to learn as they read. They must be engaged in thinking while reading so they do not simply focus on words, but rather focus on the meaning of the words in that particular context.

The during-reading techniques are based on the assertion that simply reading words is not reading. This statement often brings to mind a student that one of us taught several years ago. This student's name was Henry. He was a beautiful oral reader. However, after reading, Henry could not restate anything that he had read nor could he explain what had happened in the passage. Henry could read the words, but he could not comprehend what he had read.

This is a problem with many students in secondary school. The students have reading fluency and a workable reading rate, but they cannot comprehend the texts or use the information as a tool. The students are not connecting personal knowledge to new ideas, and they are not connecting the meaning of sentences and paragraphs to a personal idea or innovative thought. Because of this, the students are not learning effectively, and they are not using literacy as a learning tool.

The objective of the during-reading concept presented in this book is to give teachers strategies to help students who struggle with reading comprehension while at the same time helping them to improve their learning of content-area concepts. The during-reading step has three goals to enhance literacy performance. The first goal is that students recognize the power of asking themselves questions during reading. The second goal is that students realize that they may need to think beyond the words to truly understand what they are reading and to learn the intended content. The third goal is that students develop personal strategies that will help them become self-sufficient readers and learners.

Questioning

The first step of the during-reading concept involves questioning. Schmoker (2007a) contends that regardless of the content, inquiry is essential to learning and thinking. He stated that learning success depends on good text material, a structured way for students to respond to the text information, and a provocative question. Allington (2001) stated that one very important strategy for reading success is question generating. He contends that students must develop questions as they read in order to engage their thinking with the text.

We think that questioning, as an inquiry process, is the root of all learning. We learn because we have a question about something. Today, many of us log onto the Internet the moment that we have a question about something. We continually seek answers to questions such as, "How do I get there?" when planning a trip or "Are there tickets available for the game?" when wanting to see our favorite team play. We also ask more important questions about finance, health, and science, such as "How can I conserve energy at home?" or, "What happened to cause bees to begin to dwindle in number?" We learn because we want to know, and whether the answers are in books or on the Internet, we typically read to find them.

The question must be the root of a learning experience for students. Two types of questions can be used to help students engage with the reading as a learning experience. We know that students are accustomed to teacher and textbook questions. Teachers can help students with reading by using some of those questions to guide students while they read. However, students must ask questions of their own while reading to develop an inquiring stance toward learning, and there are instructional strategies that can help students learn to do this.

Students must begin to see the teacher, textbook, and self-developed questions as tools that help in mastering the information in their reading. If students see questions as a device for helping them to understand what words are saying, they will develop a skill necessary for work and for scoring well on high-stakes tests, while at the same time learning more content material and developing their comprehension ability.

While the struggling reader is the one who needs the most work with questioning when reading, all students need to learn that reading requires inquiry strategies. When students are asked to find information or to learn new information, they need to formulate an approach that will help them facilitate the process. Reading and learning from written text requires knowing what to look for in the text and knowing how to find what is in the text. This means that students need to attack reading with two questions: "What I am trying to learn?" and "What questions do I have that will help me find what I am trying to learn?"

Students should learn how to seek specific information and ideas through teacher-developed questions, and they should learn to create ideas and thoughts by developing their own questions as they read. The objective is that over time, the teacher-created questions will diminish and the student-created questions will become a strategy that students will use in reading. We want students to learn to use questions as the impetus for processing information. We believe that students can learn to devise questions that can lead them to learning essential information. We also believe that this method will lead students to better synthesize information so that they can create analytical and evaluative thoughts about the text.

Teachers can help students develop the skill of finding essential information in written documents. This can be done by providing students with directed-reading questions. These questions are designed to lead students to specific information while they read. The directed-reading questions should not be questions that only lead students to a litany of sequential facts found in a particular reading; rather, they should also lead to a synthesis of the information. The questions should lead to some specific, essential facts and develop new understanding from the reading.

Since these directed-reading questions are written so that students engage in answering the questions as they read, the teacher needs to break down the belief that a question's only purpose is to test students after they read. Students need to learn that questions can be used to guide their thinking throughout the reading. Students also need to learn that questions should be presented prior to reading and that the questions may be answered as they read. At the same time, they need to learn that they may be forming new questions as part of the process of reading.

For example, Gail Parsons, a Spanish teacher, required her students to answer some very specific questions to guide their reading. She found that students must use the reading material to find specified information that relates to what they are learning. Gail required her students to answer questions while they read in order to engage this knowledge while they were reading.

In the sample of her during-reading questions shown in Figure 4.1, Gail asked very literal questions—with the exception of question number eight. In number eight, she asked students to recount what happened in the description of a bullfight. Her intent with these questions was to focus on facts and activities that must be understood in order for students to learn about bullfighting and its impact on Spanish culture. She used these directed-reading questions to ensure that students have at least read for the information that will be necessary to learning the basic information in this unit.

Figure 4.1   Directed Reading Questions With Specific Search for Information

1. How many provinces/autonomous communities does Spain have?
   _____

2. King _____ and Queen _____ occupy the throne in Spain.

3. Spain has _____ main rivers.

4. Who started bullfighting (answers can vary)? _____
   _____
   _____

5. Bullfighting started as entertainment in _____, and then the _____ were the first to foster it as a sport.

6. The first bullfight on American soil took place in _____.

7. Bullfights are divided into _____ parts.

8. Briefly explain what happens during a bullfight. _____
   _____
   _____

9. If the judge thinks that the fight was good, what does the matador get?
   _____
   _____

Some teachers have told us that they do not like to use the type of directed-reading questions that lead to literal and specific answers. They argue that this type of question leads students to simply look through the written information to find answers. We realize that when a teacher uses directed-reading questions that are so specific, students may simply search for answers. However, by using even these clearly specified questions, the students must read something in order to find the answers. It is more effective, though, to use questions that require students to delve more deeply into the reading. When questions require students to use analysis, synthesis, and evaluation, they must focus on using their investigation and thinking skills, and this is the purpose of reading to learn.

Nicole Fink's example at the beginning of this chapter shows that she used during-reading questions regularly. She felt that if the students did not have some direction in what to look for, they would see the words as a mass of information and would be unable to process the essential meaning. Nicole used the questions in Figure 4.2 when teaching a unit on force and pressure to help students navigate their textbook reading.

With the first three questions, Nicole directed the students to the page where the information would be found. She did this as a directive to aid students in locating the information that she felt was important to learn. In order for her students to have early success in the process of questioning, she provided some specific fact questions that were easy to locate. Then, she provided questions that required more than just seeking specific answers. For example, she gave students questions (notice questions 10–12) that required students to solve mathematical problems and draw graphic illustrations. These questions provided opportunities for the students to use the information that was included in the text material and to think beyond the facts given.

Students can and should create their own questions that will aid in the during-reading step. In his lesson, Marty Christian, an automotive technology teacher, started this process by giving each student a copy of a journal article about voltage and electrical distribution in a car. He told the students to scan the article and pay close attention to the pictures. After the scanning process, he told students to close their journal and write a question about the pictures they had noticed.

Marty then put the students into small groups to share the questions they had written about the pictures. He told each group to develop one question that they all agreed was a question of particular interest for all the group members. He asked each group to tell the entire class

Figure 4.2   Directed Reading Questions for a Science Lesson on Force and
Pressure

What Is Pressure? (p. 78)

  1. Is it true or false that pressure is a type of force exerted on a surface?

Force and Pressure (p. 79)

  2. Compare the amount of pressure exerted by a force of 200 N on a 2-cm-
diameter drill bit to a force of 200 N on a 1-cm drill bit.

Calculating Pressure (pp. 79–80)

  3. What is the mathematical relationship between force, pressure, and
area?

  4. _____ is equal to the force exerted on a surface divided
by the total area over which the force is exerted.

  5. Write the equation that summarizes Newton's second law of motion.

  6. Force is measured in _____.

  7. 1 N = 1 _____ × 1 _____.

  8. _____ measures the size of the region enclosed by a
shape.

  9. Area is measured in _____ units.

 10. Compute the area of a 4-ft by 8-ft piece of plywood.

 11. Draw a diagram that illustrates the differences between the diameter and
radius of a circle.

 12. Compute the area of a 4-in PVC pipe.

the question they found most interesting, and he wrote their questions on the board. Then, he asked the students to read the entire article and focus on answering the questions on the board that had come from the groups as well as their own individual questions they had written while scanning. He also directed them to think about resources for answering any questions they had that were not answered through the reading of this article.

In this instructional strategy, Marty relied on student questioning and thinking to engage the students through the article. Through this process of having the students create questions, they learn that questions are so very important to the process of reading and comprehension. Marty said that when he uses this strategy, he finds students are more attentive to their reading because they want to answer the questions that they themselves developed. Through this process, he finds that the students have a level of curiosity prior to reading and are very focused during reading to find the information about which they are curious.

All three of these teachers' questioning techniques allow the students the option of answering the questions either as they read or after they have read the material. This instructional strategy is designed to ensure that students are seeking information and ideas as they read. Also, this strategy is used so that students interact with the words they are reading. These teachers never simply assign reading; they engage students in activities through questioning that guide their thinking as they read.

Another way to engage students in reading through questions is to teach them about the research process while having them read. Steve Shadel, a science teacher, uses online exploration as a way for students to read and research. In a lesson on the physics of momentum, Steve placed students into small groups. He then provided them with a series of brief reading activities that were available on the Internet. With each reading, he required students to engage in activities that would demonstrate that they had read the material he assigned on each Web site. The lesson structure is found in Figure 4.3.

There are several critical points about the during-reading experience in this lesson. First, Steve directed students to read information from varied Web sites in the process of learning about momentum. Second, he expected students to work collaboratively so that they could discuss what they were reading as they worked on the problems they were expected to complete. A third crucial activity was that he required students to use the information immediately. The students were *doing* as they were reading.

Figure 4.3   A Physics Lesson Requiring Online Reading

MOMENTUM AND IMPULSE

Linear Momentum

Go to the Web site below and fill in the equation.

http://id.mind.net/%7Ezona/mstm/physics/mechanics/momentum/introductory
Problems/momentumSummary1.html

> Momentum equals _____ times _____.

Now complete the three "Related Problems." **Show work!**

1.

2.

3.

Impulse

http://id.mind.net/%7Ezona/mstm/physics/mechanics/momentum/introductory
Problems/momentumSummary2.html

> _____ applied over _____
>
> create _____.

The Impulse		**The Change**

Now complete the five "Related Problems" indicated using the equation above.
Show work!

4.

5.

6.

7.

8.

http://www.physicsclassroom.com/Class/momentum/U4L1b.html

Complete the chart.

#	Force (N)	Time (sec)	Impulse (N·sec)	ΔP (kg·m/sec)	Mass (kg)	Δv (m/s)
1		0.010			10	−4
2		0.100	−40		10	
3		0.010		−200	50	
4	−20,000			−200		−8
5	−200	1.0			50	

Conservation of Momentum Misconceptions

http://www.regentsprep.org/Regents/physics/phys01/miscons/default.htm

State the "bad physics" shown and explain why it is not realistic.

Conservation of Momentum

http://id.mind.net/%7Ezona/mstm/physics/mechanics/momentum/introductory
Problems/momentumSummary6.html

Now do the "Related Problem" indicated. **Show work!**

9.

Figure 4.3 (Continued)

Collisions

http://www.regentsprep.org/Regents/physics/phys01/colitype/default.htm

Fill in the table below for the two major types of collisions.

Collision Type	List _Two_ Properties or Characteristics	One Example
	• •	
	• •	

When teachers ask students to focus on questions while reading, students learn the importance of using questions as a device that will lead to greater understanding. The purpose of directing students to use questions while reading is to lead them to actively seek specific information. This gives them practice using questions as a comprehending strategy during reading. Students, however, must develop the skill of posing self-developed questions that will lead to self-sufficiency as readers.

One process students can use is that of writing questions while they read. David Garnes, an English teacher, suggests that the best way to have students write questions when they are reading is to use a sticky-note method. He gives students a packet of sticky notes and asks students to write questions on them that come to their minds while reading. He then instructs the students to place the questions on the page near the section of text where the question arose.

With this method, students can easily find the place in the text where they had a question. The use of sticky notes alleviates the problem that can develop if students are marking the margins or underlining in textbooks owned by the school. The students still have a direct connection to where a question was developed, and more important, the students are directly interacting with the text.

In our work, we met David Wolinsky, a high school science teacher. David also uses this sticky-note method. However, David decided to use this method because he discovered that when he used a highly structured set of directed-reading questions with his stronger readers, they appeared stifled by the need to simply answer the questions and did not seek out further information. So he worked with his students to ask their own questions as they read.

David learned that students need to learn how to ask questions that go beyond those with one-word answers or one sequential group of words in the text. Because of this, he established a rule: "If your question can be answered with one word or with a group of words written on the page where you are reading, the answer should be committed to memory. If you cannot find the answer in one word or one group of words, you may write the question and stick it in your book. If you write a question and, after reading further, you discover a one-word answer or one group of words that answers the question, you must mark the page where the answer is found on your sticky note with the question and leave the note on the page where you originally placed it."

David wanted students to see that some questions could be answered directly as the reader proceeded through a text but that not all information is found on the page where the question came to mind. His rationale was that students would have concrete evidence of how reading can work. The reader may have a question stimulated at one point and the information regarding the question may come later—the reader must continue reading in order to find the answers to their questions.

He now finds that this method has stimulated quite a bit of discussion and a deeper search for full understanding of the concepts found in biology. He says that more of his students become involved in class discussions and that the students can always reference where the question was developed and then where the response to the question was found. This gives all students the opportunity to reread a passage as they delve into the depths of a concept. These activities show students that seeking information while reading and developing their own thinking along the way are both part of the reading process.

We caution teachers that using either teacher-directed or student self-developed questions can lead students to just find concrete answers to questions if they do not learn to develop questions that require thinking. In order to develop questions at varied levels of thinking, teachers and students can use a tool, the Shikellamy Verb Matrix (Perna & Davis, 2006). By using the verb matrix, teachers and students can readily review action verbs that can stimulate question development for thinking beyond the knowledge level. This Verb Matrix, shown in Figure 4.4, can stimulate the teacher to mull over several choices of verbs that correspond with the knowledge, comprehension, application, analysis, synthesis, and evaluation levels of understanding. As the teachers contemplate the matrix, they can seek

Figure 4.4   Verb Matrix Developed by Shikellamy School District, Sunbury, PA

Know: A student knows when the student can communicate information or complete a learning activity without reference to external sources.

Trigger Verbs: Identify   List   Name   State   Write

Comprehend: A student comprehends when the student demonstrates the nature, significance, or meaning of information by presenting the information in his or her own words.

Trigger Verbs: Calculate   Restate   Explain   Illustrate   Predict

Apply: A student applies learned information when the student can utilize the information in the process of solving a problem or creating a concept.

Trigger Verbs: Relate   Use   Utilize   Employ   Demonstrate

Analyze: A student analyzes when the student can separate the various details within a piece of information and can communicate how each detail relates to other details to form the piece of information.

Trigger Verbs: Deduce   Dissect/Examine   Break down   Compare/Contrast

Synthesize: A student synthesizes when the student creates an idea by composing several parts and elements into one piece of information.

Trigger Verbs: Combine   Compose   Create   Develop   Construct

Evaluate: A student evaluates when a student can present information that supports why he or she places the value or significance on pieces of information.

Trigger Verbs: Appraise   Assess   Rate   Judge   Determine

Source: Used with permission of the Shikellamy School District, Sunbury, Pennsylvania.

to raise the expectations of students in answering teacher-developed directed-reading questions by using an action verb from the matrix to compose a question corresponding to higher-level thinking. The verb matrix can be explained and its use demonstrated to students so they can also use it as a tool when composing their own questions.

Jigsawing Text and Graphic Organizers

Other practices beyond questioning can engage reading, thinking, and comprehension skills. One way to do this is to ask students to use *jigsawing*, where different students each read a portion of a complete reading and teach their part to others in the class. Through this process, students become experts on their section of text. During the reading, their focus is on determining important points to share with others who have not read their section. Often, several students will read a section and meet together to discuss their understanding before sharing their section of text with the whole class. This way, the amount of text to be read is not overwhelming and each person has the opportunity to be an expert. In addition, by teaching others about their section, students must summarize and synthesize what they have read.

Another important practice is the use of graphic organizers. Students can visually represent the information in the text as they read, which engages their thinking during the reading process (Duke & Pearson, 2002). In Figure 4.5, Rick Miles, a building construction teacher, takes his students through several steps in a reading experience about roof styles. The during-reading step of the lesson is based on both the jigsawing of the reading and the use of graphic organizers.

Rick used graphic organizers and jigsaw reading in small sections as part of this reading experience. His purpose was for students to learn the different types of roof styles. He was not concerned that all students read every word in the entire book section. Because his purpose was gaining knowledge about roof styles, he chunked the reading into smaller sections and had the students share their learning in a jigsaw process. He gave small groups assigned reading, and he gave each group activities that engaged the students while they were reading the textual material. With jigsawing, the students who have difficulty reading or who are slower readers did not find the assignment too challenging and were more willing to attempt to read the smaller section assigned to them.

Beyond the jigsawing, this experience required students to think organizationally by using graphic organizers. As Strangman and

Figure 4.5   A Building Construction Class During-Reading Experience on Roof Styles

Before Reading

Step 1: The teacher told students to do a "quick look" of the textbook section on roof styles. He told the students that they have three minutes to scan through the entire section.

Step 2: The teacher asked students if they had questions about what they noticed in the scanning and posted questions on a chart at the front of the room.

During Reading

Step 3: The teacher divided the class into groups of three students. He assigned a section of pages that covered two types of roof styles to each group. The teacher told each student group that they were responsible for reading their assigned pages and reporting the information back to the entire class.

Step 4: The teacher gave each group the two graphic organizers shown below. He told the students that as they read they must list the name of a roof style in each middle circle of the organizer. The teacher then told the students to write characteristics about the roof style in each of the extending characteristics circles.

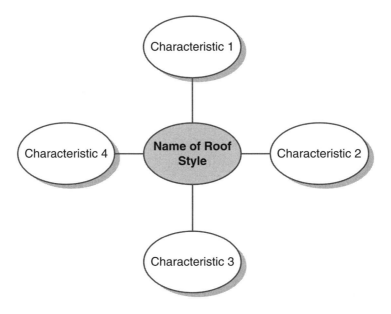

Step 5: The teacher told the students to do their reading and fill in the chart as they read.

After Reading

Step 6: The teacher told the students to end their reading and that they had two minutes to compare their charts and pick a person to report to the class.

Step 7: The teacher then gave the groups two graphic organizers like the one below.

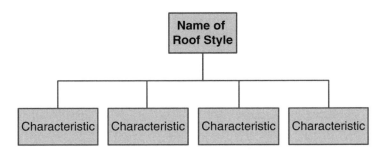

Step 8: The teacher told the groups to use the graphic organizers to identify the roof style that they read about and list four characteristics about the style.

Hall (2004) stated, graphic organizers help students to see the relationships between facts, terms, and ideas within a learning task. Rick set up a situation where students must interact with the reading and organize their thoughts. The students must clearly find information and identify the information in a pattern that will help them understand how terms and facts fit together.

A key to the during-reading step is that students need to make personal connections with the words in the text, and they need to make mental connections between ideas or facts within the text (Beuhl, n.d.). Rick Miles makes this happen by having students find specific details about the varied types of roof styles. He also provides students with graphic organizers that require students to connect descriptors to the main type of roof. Basically, he sets up a way for students to develop well-organized thinking with the graphic organizers (from which students can write more systematic notes).

Reciprocal Teaching

The during-learning experience can involve students working together on concepts as they read. One example is reciprocal teaching, which is defined as a dialogue about a text (Palinscar & Brown, 1984). This dialogue occurs while the reading takes place. The four key ideas are summarizing, question generating, clarifying, and predicting. The method can involve the teacher leading the dialogue with students using the four key ideas. After practicing with the teacher as the leader, the teacher turns the dialogue over to the students, and they continue the practice in small groups in the classroom.

J. R. Holenchik used this method with his students. He assigned students a passage in a novel. He placed his students in small groups where each person was responsible for one of the four key ideas used in reciprocal teaching. One student developed a brief summary of the passage. Another student was responsible for creating a series of questions about the passage. A third student was required to develop clarification about vocabulary or a confusing text passage. The fourth student made a list of predictions about what could happen later in the novel. Each student in the group had a particular focus to guide his or her reading.

The next day, after the reading assignment was completed, each student reported back to all students in the group about his or her particular focus. This brief discussion of the focus areas in the small groups led to much stronger whole-class discussion because all people in the group had an understanding of the passage.

Think-Alouds

We have also seen secondary teachers use a think-aloud method. After the teacher has modeled aloud how to think through reading passages, the teacher encourages students to ask themselves questions, comment to themselves about something that they have read, or predict out loud what will happen in the text. Beers (2003) contended that students need to talk so that they can stay focused on the meaning of the thoughts. She suggests that putting students into groups and allowing them to talk while taking turns reading helps the students give consideration to prediction possibilities, questions, or comments about confusing sections.

We saw successful use of thinking and talking aloud in an algebra class. Thomas Boito encouraged students to read word problems aloud. Sometimes, he told students to read the problem out loud and listen for the essential information as they heard themselves read. At other times, he placed the class in paired groups and told one student to read the problem aloud while the partner restated out loud what the problem was about in his or her own words. Thomas used this strategy because he found that students needed opportunities to think while hearing the problem, rather than just reading it to themselves. By taking away the cognitive issues surrounding the act of reading, the listener could focus on the content of the problem.

Thomas also took the think-aloud, talk-aloud system to a new arena when he used it with traditional number and symbol problems in math. He paired the students and told them to read the problem. If symbols were used in the problem, he wanted the students to speak out loud what the symbol was. For example, if the students saw $a^2 + b^2 = c^2$, the students were expected to say to each other, "There is a plus, an equal, and three square root signs in the problem." He then told the students to go one more step. Instead of thinking in terms of a, b, and c, he told them to give names to a, b, and c. In the problem presented here, the students were working with the Pythagorean theorem, so the students could say length of the wall on my right and length of the wall on my left is equal to the length of the line running from the top corner on my right to the lower corner on my left. Thomas finds that many students cannot do math work without thinking in words, so he uses this talk-aloud system to help them configure the language necessary for the mathematics work.

Oral Reading

One of the points that we want to make concerning the during-reading step relates to the concept of oral reading. We recommend that teachers selectively choose times when students and teachers orally read to the class. We do not dispute the evidence that oral reading is useful for young children for the development of fluency and for teacher monitoring of reading processes. However, we believe that in secondary schools, oral reading by the teacher or round-robin reading by students does not encourage active engagement with the reading material. Some teachers in our pilot schools discovered that when they read to the students, the students would not focus with them unless the reading was very brief and the teacher posed questions immediately prior to reading the passage. One other point that a teacher made to us in his review of the use of oral reading was simply, "It is difficult to do a dramatic reading of the introduction of a mathematics procedure. The students were bored. I was bored."

In this chapter, we have defined some very important aspects of the during-reading procedure. First, we suggested that questions as part of an inquiry process are the root of learning. By having questions to engage thinking while reading, students have a greater chance of learning. Second, we suggested that students need to be engaged and thinking while they read. If students know that they are to have questions or are developing questions while they read, they will have a stronger interaction with the words. Third, we suggested that students must move beyond simply finding answers as they read. In everything from placing questions on sticky notes to doing a scavenger hunt through the textbook, students must work to understand how components of the text fit together and do not stand alone as singular entities. The fourth concept that we think makes this a positive method for the during-reading experience is structure. The students are not simply told to "read the chapter." Students are given structured activities that merge with the reading of the text material. It is these activities that help students to solidify knowledge and lead to more in-depth thinking about the material. When the students practice these levels of thinking with their reading, they are learning to learn.

5

After Reading

Postreading activities are as varied as the teachers with whom we worked, and several teachers focused on writing as the key to postreading activity. Sue Hetrick, a physical education teacher, and Eric Bergmueller, a music teacher, both said that writing after learning helped their students solidify their comprehension.

Sue required students to complete journals in which they wrote substantive descriptions to open-ended questions, such as "How would you describe your activity level today?" As the year went along, she expected deeper descriptions than comments such as "Real difficult" or "I worked real hard." She said she expected students to use good grammar and strong sentence structure in order to clearly demonstrate that they thought about the reading and learning experiences in the class.

Eric showed us student journals in which they wrote reactions to open-ended questions about their guitar performances of a song from the 1970s called "A Horse With No Name." In his questions, Eric asked students to reflect on what they had done while practicing to perform the song. He asked them such questions as "When you demonstrated your skill to another person, what was that person's reaction?" Another question was, "When you talked with a classmate, did the classmate's experience compare to your experience?"

Eric's intention with these questions was to find out if students could specifically relate to things they had learned while going through the learning process. He wanted them to demonstrate an understanding of the vocabulary and concepts that had been taught when the lesson was delivered. He contends that when students are expected to use the vocabulary and state the concepts that were part of the lesson, the students retain the information well beyond the time period of instruction.

One fascinating postreading experience we came across involved an approach used by Bernadette Boerckel. She approached postreading by asking students to think about what they had read, heard, or seen. She required students to find one sentence that best summed up the general concept or meaning of what they read. In her own words, Bernadette explains the impact of this process:

> I ask students to write down one sentence that *best* sums up the general meaning of the text as a whole—the passage that is essential to the text. This is difficult for them at first, but encourages close reading, synthesis, comprehension, and thesis identification.
>
> In my experience, here is what tends to happen in a class: The first time I get ten to fifteen different quotes from the class. I hear them all and we discuss why each was chosen and eventually come to an agreement on the best few. Each subsequent attempt produces more and more initial class agreement until, after a half dozen or so experiences, most of the class comes in with the same one or two essential passages. What is so energizing about this approach is, as a teacher, I can't lose! When students' quotes do not agree, they argue for (defend) their quote—thus provoking great class discussion that is completely text based. When the students do agree, I have evidence that I am helping them to become careful readers. (Bernadette Boerckel, personal communication)

We think that Bernadette's method helps students to develop an essential quality for learning. As opposed to trying to remember every word or idea, the students must analytically formulate a summation of the reading. This summation is critical to learning. After all, students cannot be expected to memorize every word that they read or hear. Instead, successful learners must use the information that they have read or heard and then summarize it into a concept that sticks with them. The students must consider what they have read. They must formulate an idea about what they have read and then use analytical thinking to determine what statement summarizes the concept.

The postreading step is not a step where students are asked to prove that they can pass a test. Instead, this part of the process is designed to involve students in activities that will engage them with the information found in the reading or learning. The student is expected to process the information and seek specific parts of the textual material to support knowledge, opinions, and new ideas. In this step of the process, students are asked to demonstrate whether they can synthesize essential information in order to show an understanding of the essence of the written material.

This process of continuing to build understanding and teaching how to comprehend is not what has been done in the past. In the past, the expectation was for students to read and then take a quiz. This "read then quiz" method leads students to believe that recall of specific facts is comprehension. Typically, the day-after-reading quiz involves questions that consist of one word or phrase. In reality, those quizzes assess memory more than they assess comprehension. Learning how to learn in a particular content area is critically important—not just simple recall of facts on a quiz or multiple-choice test.

Schank (n.d.) supported this thinking when he explained that many teachers are stifling student learning by asking one-answer questions as an assessment of reading comprehension. He contends that questions with one-word answers do not require students to think and synthesize the information that they have read. Schmoker (2006) concurred with Schank. He pointed out that, in his observations of schools, he saw 52% of teachers using worksheets that assessed recall of words and phrases to demonstrate comprehension of learning, while only 3% of classrooms showed evidence of higher-order thinking to assess comprehension.

When we first observed teachers in the schools where we worked, we found this information to be relatively true. Teachers focused mainly on content facts and posed questions that could be answered by one word or term that could easily be found in the assigned reading. In one example, a science teacher asked us to observe because he was going to use small-group activities. The teacher had designed a game in the form of *Jeopardy*, where teams worked together to review a reading assignment. After we observed, the teacher told us how he used this game to encourage group activity and to assess comprehension of what the students had learned. While the teacher thought he was encouraging group interaction, we saw the teacher pose one-word or phrase statements for which students could create knowledge-based questions. The first student who remembered the answer blurted out a question without reference to fellow team members, and there was no need to process information since the single-word or phrase answers required little processing of information. The questions being formed for the *Jeopardy*-like answer were at the knowledge level.

The idea that the teacher wanted students to know certain information was not a negative in itself, but the students were simply reacting to bits of information that did not indicate higher-level comprehension. We believe that postreading activities must provide opportunities for students to explore information as the teacher facilitates synthesis, analysis, and evaluation experiences. If students have learned things that are different from what the teacher has ascertained that the students should learn, the teacher must help the students make the mental connections that will lead them to the important information. At the same time, when students are given the opportunity to share what they have learned, they may help each other create the connections necessary to comprehend essential information.

Stiggins (2005) said that knowledge is a foundation of learning. He maintains that when pieces of knowledge are connected, learning occurs. This means that some of the postreading experiences must lead students to demonstrate that they have gathered some specific knowledge in order to learn further information. This basic knowledge is the foundation for higher-level thinking, not the end point.

One way to examine essential information is through a review of key points that are made in a reading selection. Nicole Fink showed how she does this through the use of an anticipation guide in a lesson on pressure that she gave her special education students. In Figure 5.1, the reader can see that Nicole gave students an anticipation guide that they used during a prereading experience. By looking back at the anticipation guide, students were able to determine whether they had changed their minds after reading the information about pressure. In doing so, the students were engaged in determining if they had a knowledge base of some of the specific information from the reading. This basic information was a building block for further work with the material.

Nicole used these building blocks as a forerunner to a course of action in which students focused on processing the newly learned information. She required students to work together to solve a series of problems. As seen in Figure 5.1, the student teams processed information as they worked through two math problems (Questions 1 and 2), and they worked on two problems that asked them to go beyond factual information. They were asked a question about creating pressure change and then had to generate a problem that required a higher level of information processing. The first of those discussion problems were somewhat traditional in that they asked students to do a traditional math problem. However, the second question led to

Figure 5.1   Lesson on Pressure

LESSON ON PRESSURE

Teacher Introductory Statement: By the end of this lesson, students will be able to define and calculate pressure in the scientific sense.

Before Reading

   Step 1: The teacher distributes the anticipation guide shown below.

Anticipation and Reaction Guide

Directions: Before reading pages 78 through 80 in the text, check the before-reading statements with *Agree* or *Disagree*. After reading, decide what the author said and check the after-reading statements with *Agree* or *Disagree*.

Anticipation Guide Before Reading		*Pressure*	*Reaction Guide After Reading*	
Agree	*Disagree*		*Agree*	*Disagree*
		1. *Pressure* is a force exerted on a surface.		
		2. You exert more pressure when you are lying down on a floor than when you are standing up.		
		3. A *newton* is a unit of force.		
		4. *Area* is the measure of the distance around the outside of an object.		
		5. The area of an object is measured in square units.		
		6. You can calculate pressure by multiplying the force exerted on a surface by the total area over which the force is exerted.		
		7. Pressure is measured in pascals.		

   Step 2: The teacher will lead a discussion with students concerning the information that they have checked on the anticipation guide. The teacher does **not** give students the correct information. She allows students to offer their opinions as to with what they agree or disagree.

(Continued)

Figure 5.1 (Continued)

Step 3: The teacher directs the students to place the Anticipation Guide into their notebooks. She explains that they will bring the guides out for further work at the end of the reading.

Step 4: The teacher distributes a set of guided reading questions to the students. A sample of those questions is shown below.

What Is Pressure? (p. 78)

1. Is it true or false that pressure is a type of force exerted on a surface?

Force and Pressure (p. 79)

2. Compare the amount of pressure exerted by a force of 200 N on a 2 cm diameter drill bit to a force of 200 N on a 1 cm drill bit.

Calculating Pressure (pp. 79–80)

3. What is the mathematical relationship between force, pressure, and area?

4. _____ is equal to the force exerted on a surface divided by the total area over which the force is exerted.

5. Write the equation that summarizes Newton's second law of motion.

6. Force is measured in _____.

7. 1 N = 1 _____ × 1 _____.

8. _____ measures the size of the region enclosed by a shape.

9. Area is measured in _____ units.

10. Compute the area of a 4-by-8-foot piece of plywood.

11. Draw a diagram that illustrates the differences between the diameter and radius of a circle.

12. Compute the area of a 4-inch PVC pipe.

Step 5: The teacher reads the directed questions to the students. She tells them that they will use these questions while completing the reading.

During Reading

Step 1: The teacher tells the students to scan the four pages that have been assigned for reading.

Step 2: The teacher tells the students to review directed reading questions one through three. She tells students to try to find the answers to the three questions by looking for the specific information needed to answer the questions.

Step 3: The teacher tells students that they will read the entire selection while she reads orally. She tells the students to place their books on one area of the desk and place the directed reading questions on another area of the desk. She tells students that she will give them time to answer directed reading questions when she has finished reading. She explains that students may mark a page number beside the questions if they realize that she has read something that can answer one of the questions.

Step 4: The teacher reads the passage aloud.

Step 5: After the oral reading, the teacher directs the students to find the necessary information to complete the directed reading questions. She then gives students time to seek the information. While the students are completing the directed reading questions, the teacher circulates and helps students who need additional guidance.

After Reading

Step 1: The teacher directs the students to locate the anticipation guide they used at the start of the lesson. She then tells students to react to the statements on the right side of the guide by putting a checkmark in the agree or disagree column.

Step 2: The teacher leads an oral review of the anticipation guide information.

Step 3: The teacher breaks the class into groups. Each group is given a problem that relates to the reading. The teacher tells the students that each group must solve their problem and that one spokesperson must offer an explanation to the class about how the problem was solved.

1. A solid block of wood has a square base of .5 m × .5 m and weighs 5000 N. How much pressure does it exert on the floor where it rests?
2. A hammer strikes a nail with a force of 100 N. If the head of a nail is 0.003 m^2, what is the pressure exerted on the nail?
3. How can you create a lower pressure? A higher pressure?
4. Generate a problem where a classmate must calculate the pressure exerted on an object.

Step 4: The teacher provides time for each group to present their problem and explain how they solved the problem. The teacher will pose pertinent questions as needed to help student comprehension.

Step 5: The teacher gives each group a laboratory experience that will help them demonstrate their understanding of pressure. The lab is shown below.

PRESSURE

Problem: Do smaller lids exert more or less pressure than larger lids?

Hypothesis:

_____

_____

(Continued)

Figure 5.1 (Continued)

Materials:

- 2 containers of modeling clay
- 2 pieces of wax paper
- Small lid
- Large lid
- 1 kg mass
- 2 kg mass
- Metric ruler

Experiment:

1. Spread a layer of modeling clay onto a sheet of wax paper.

2. Place the small lid on the modeling clay, set the 1-kg mass on top, and observe the modeling clay's appearance after 5 seconds.

3. Calculate the amount of pressure exerted on the small lid.

4. Spread another layer of modeling clay onto the second sheet of wax paper.

5. Place the large lid on the modeling clay, set the 1-kg mass on top, and observe the modeling clay's appearance after 5 seconds.

6. Calculate the amount of pressure exerted on the large lid.

7. Repeat Steps 1 through 6 using the 2-kg mass.

Data:

Lid Size	Force (N)	Area (m²)	Pressure (Pa)
Small			
Large			
Small			
Large			

Conclusion:

_____

_____

Source: Developed by Nicole Fink, special education teacher.

interesting discussions because students had to make two decisions. First, the group had to determine what object they wanted to use. Second, they needed to use knowledge from their reading to determine how to pose a question to generate a problem.

Graphic Organizers

Part of postreading experiences must involve having students reflect on specific information that is critical to a segment of written discourse. Marzano (2007) indicated that graphic organizers are popular ways to input information in order to demonstrate knowledge. Michelle Twiddy required her students to use a plot diagram as a graphic organizer throughout a lesson to help them understand literary terms. In Michelle's lesson (Figure 5.2), she wanted students to learn specific information, but she also asked them to organize this information in a graphic that helped them understand the terms and text structure involved in narratives.

In Steps 4 and 5 of her postreading experience, Michelle helped students solidify their basic knowledge by using the graphic organizer as a familiar pattern within which to list the basic key-word knowledge that they had developed in their pre- and postreading activities. In Step 5, she required the students to work together to come up with written statements about what each term meant. Michelle realized that her goal was for students to go beyond memorizing definitions. She wanted the students to develop definitions that would become working knowledge because the meanings of the terms would be connected to their own thinking. To help the students do this, she directed them to work in teams to develop written definitions placed alongside the key term in the graphic organizer.

A key element in Michelle's lesson was having the students work together to develop their own written definition for each term. She did not want the students to use purely memorized phrases in defining the terms. Instead, she wanted the students to have a working knowledge of the terminology framed within their own thinking. By having the students work together to develop their own written definition for the term, Michelle encouraged students to think about the meaning, discuss the term, and put their thoughts into a written statement. Because the students in this example understood the terms involved in narrative plot structure, they were able to use this graphic organizer to better understand narrative.

This process is based on the idea that postreading activities must engage students as they interact with information. Students must feel free to discuss and react to what they have read. Most important, the students must be willing to share what they have learned. By sharing what they have learned, students can process the information in order to establish a stronger understanding of the material.

Figure 5.2   Graphic Organizer for Literary Terms

LESSON ON PLOT DIAGRAM ACTIVITY

Teacher Introductory Statement: By the end of this lesson, you will have a sense of how to use a plot diagram to identify six parts of a plot.

Before Reading

Step 1: The teacher tells the students that there are several words or terms that are very important to this lesson. She states each word or term and provides a definition.

Plot: The events in the story; has an identifiable beginning, middle, and end

Plot Diagram: The events in the story laid out in a given format

Exposition: The introduction of the characters, setting, and conflict

Situation (initial incident): A problem, conflict, or mystery that gets the story rolling; background information

Rising Action: The events that develop the conflict and characters

Climax: The highest, most exciting point of the story; the point to which all the rising action builds

Falling Action: The events leading up to the final closure of the plot

Resolution (denouement): The event(s) that wraps up the situation

Step 2: The teacher tells the students that they have two minutes to quickly look through the pages of Chapter 4 in the "Measuring Up to the Pennsylvania Academic Standards" (PSSA) Level H.

Step 3: The teacher asks the students to write any questions that they have after they have completed their quick glance through the material to be read.

Step 4: The teacher asks students to state some of their questions. She tells the students that these questions will be answered during the reading or after the reading has been completed and that they have the information necessary to compose answers to their questions.

Step 5: The teacher distributes a model of a plot line. The model that she gives to students includes the teacher's personal definitions of the terms found on a plot line. The model was shown within the reading passage that the students had quickly scanned. The model with the teacher definitions is shown below.

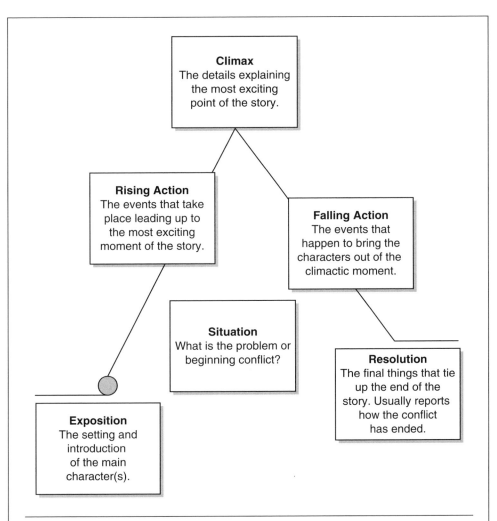

Source: Adapted from Chapter 4 in the "Measuring Up to the Pennsylvania Academic Standards" (PSSA) Level H, pp. 175–181, published by Peoples Publishing Group, copyright 2002.

Step 6: The teachers tells the students that they have one minute to review the model. She informs the students that they will be required to place this model in their work folders after the cursory one-minute scan.

Step 7: The teacher tells the students to place the model in their notebooks and not to refer to it while they read.

During Learning

Step 1: The teacher tells students to open their books to Chapter 4 in the "Measuring Up to the Pennsylvania Academic Standards" (PSSA) Level H, page 175.

(Continued)

Figure 5.2 (Continued)

Step 2: The teacher tells students to do another quick look at this chapter.

Step 3: The teacher refers to the questions that students asked earlier when they did a quick review of the chapter. She shows those questions on the board in front of the room and reads them orally.

Step 4: The teacher distributes a worksheet like the one below.

Chapter 4 Note Sheet

Question	Notes, Thoughts, and Questions That You Have While Learning
1	
2	
3	
4	
5	

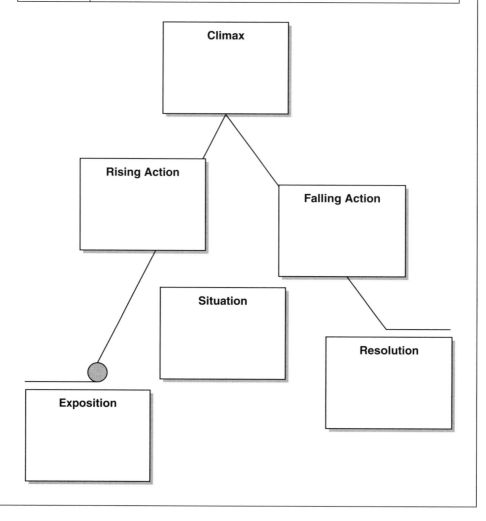

Step 5: The teacher tells the students that while they read they are to answer the questions on the note sheet. She says that they may answer the questions as they read or take notes while they read and develop their answers after they have read the material. Regardless of when they answer the questions, they must answer the questions in sentence form.

Step 6: The teacher tells the students that they must use the graphic organizer to make notes about each segment in the plot line. She tells the students that they must have something noted in each box. She explains that they may write a definition or simply write notes.

Step 7: The teacher circulates through the room while the students read and answers any questions while the students complete the graphic organizer.

After Reading

Step 1: The teacher directs all students to submit their worksheets to her.

Step 2: The teacher distributes the plot line graphic organizer again. This time there are no names or terms in the cells. The organizer looks like the one below.

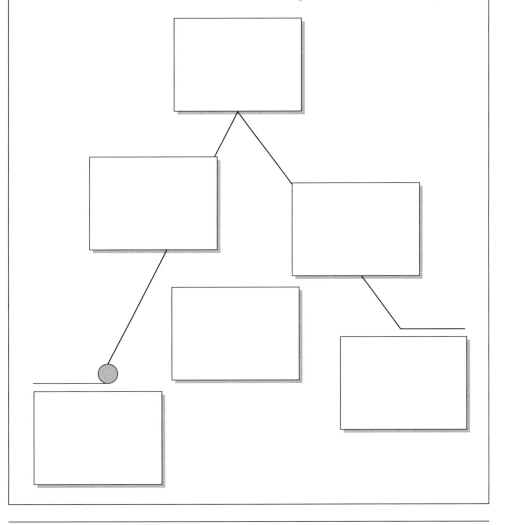

Figure 5.2 (Continued)

Step 3: The teacher breaks the students into groups of three. There are four copies of the blank graphic organizer for each group. She directs the groups to work together and use their memories. She tells the students that they have five to seven minutes to work together on one of the organizers. She tells the students to fill in the cells of the organizer with the proper terms in the sequence that they have seen as they remember it from work that they have previously done.

Step 4: The teacher leads a brief discussion with the students about what they have placed on the blank graphic organizer. The teacher works with the class to reach consensus as to what words fit in which cell. The teacher ultimately is sure that the proper terms fit in each cell. She tells students to fill out their individual blank graphic organizers with the appropriate terms in the proper sequence.

Step 5: The teacher directs students to pull out the sheet that they used to take notes during the reading of the passage. She organizes the class into groups again and tells them to discuss their notes on the components. She tells the students to develop a group consensus as to how to define each component.

Step 6: The teacher gives the students a few minutes to discuss what they have learned.

Step 7: The teacher leads a discussion toward a final definition for each term in the plot sequence. As the students come very close to the teacher-expected definition, the teacher says, "That is correct. Let's write it down in the cell on the graphic organizer." She continues leading this process until all terms are identified in the cells.

Words I do not know	After I read, what do I think the word means?
Questions that I thought of as I scanned	After I read, what are my answers to these questions?

Source: Developed by Michelle Twiddy, English teacher.

Written Summaries

Summarization is one way to demonstrate that a reader or learner has comprehended what has been read; it is also an opportunity for students to develop their thinking. However, summarization must be done in a way that requires students to process the information as opposed to simply trying to list everything that was written in the passage. As Allington (2001) pointed out, people are asked to summarize as a routine activity in life. They are asked to tell others what they have read in a newspaper, what they saw in a movie, or what happened at a game. People do not want a long dissertation that demonstrates that the reader remembered every detail. Instead, they want to know the essence of the news article, the movie, or what happened at a game. The person who can summarize well has the ability to point out the essential points that can create a picture for the person asking the question.

Summaries are most effectively done when students are required to write their summary. The use of written summaries is effective because the students have to determine the important ideas and organize those ideas in a meaningful sequence as they write. This requires more thinking than a simple listing of factual information and allows for more in-depth thinking than can be done orally. In addition, written summaries let the teacher know if students have internalized the important concepts they are supposed to learn.

Cosmas Curry asked students to write brief summaries both to guide student thinking and to determine if they comprehended concepts in his driver-education classes. In this postreading experience, he gave students a small-group activity to help them process and discuss some of the information in the readings they were required to do. For example, he often instructed students to discuss and compare answers to directed-reading questions as a part of their postreading activity. However, the focus of these postreading experiences was individual writing. Cosmas found that he had a great deal of success with one basic activity. He told students to write five sentences that identified the five most important things they had learned in the lesson. He asked that the sentences be complete and structurally sound so that he could understand what the writer was explaining. He collected each student's five sentences and reviewed them prior to the next class time.

At the start of the next lesson, Cosmas returned the five sentences to the students. He told them to review the sentences and read any notes he may have placed on the papers. Then, he asked the students to take a few minutes to turn their sentences into a paragraph. He wanted the students to summarize their learning from the previous day. Cosmas suggests that this two-step approach to writing a summary has helped students engage in thinking about what they have learned and also has helped the students solidify their comprehension about what they have read in the lesson.

Along with using summarizing to solidify understanding and learning, there is an assessment perspective to this activity. Cosmas used the group activity to process student thinking, but he worked with individuals when he assessed the students' writing about their own learning. As opposed to the traditional class discussion where only a small number of students may become actively involved in a discussion, Cosmas made sure that all students in the class provided evidence that they understood the reading through the written summaries.

High school teachers have said that they have students who do not read or write well enough to do written summaries. However, there is strong evidence to support written responses to reading. Elbow (1994) told us that many times students can provide the one-word answer to a question but still not know the information in a contextual sense. This is an idea that Cosmas learned by using the summary paragraphs as a conclusion to a unit. He found that when he had students write summary paragraphs, they seemed to have a stronger working knowledge of the driver-education concepts. He told us that more students had a contextual knowledge of the concepts and could refer to these concepts in subsequent lessons.

The Importance of Writing

Cosmas has used writing both as an assessment tool and as a learning tool. The fact that students seemed to remember contextual information in future classes indicated that the writing functioned as a learning tool. Fisher and Frey (2007) capitalized on Elbow's (1994) theory that writing can work as a learning tool. They presented the premise that writing is thinking on paper and that the use of writing helps students to clarify their thinking and thereby enhance their learning. Their conclusion was that if students write about what they have read, they will develop a higher level of comprehension because the placing of words on paper makes the student compose their thoughts into a defined interpretation of what they have read.

The more students write as part of their postreading experiences, the greater the chance of two things occurring. First, the act of writing helps solidify learning, and writing itself can help reading skill. In one technical school where we worked, the students' writing scores increased at the same time that reading scores increased. Smith (2001) pointed out the important connection between reading and writing processes because both create meaning through text. Students must read in order to become readers and students must write in order to become comfortable using words and developing meaning. As students learn to develop their thoughts through written discourse, they can more readily understand what they read. They can better understand how texts are put together and the contextual frameworks of written language.

Even though any form of writing can help students develop thinking skills, writing during the postreading period must involve using information from the reading to substantiate the written thoughts. In order for students to develop strong comprehension skills, they must see how to synthesize knowledge in the reading with their own personal thoughts and with knowledge found outside the reading. As McConachie et al. (2006) stated, "Knowledge and thinking must go hand in hand" (p. 8).

One of the teachers we observed used postreading and learning experiences as a time for students to use writing as preparation for a project. Steve Younkers, a construction-trades teacher, was firm in his belief that students must use writing as a part of developing comprehension. Steve required all students to write job specifications for their small building projects that followed textbook theory lessons. He focused his prereading on vocabulary development in the traditional sense and gave students a list of terms to learn. During the lesson's reading assignment, he provided directed-reading questions that students were to answer as they read.

Following a reading assignment, Steve placed the students in groups and had them review their answers to the directed-reading questions. He functioned as the expert by offering more definitive information as the groups discussed and reported their answers. For example, if students did not have a clear response to one of the directed-reading questions, Steve offered comments that led the group to more useful information. He asked each group to develop any other questions that they may have had about the textbook material. He required that the groups work together to compose written questions and that each student write the questions on a piece of paper. His contention was that when all students were required to write down questions, more students got involved in the discussion and processed some of the information necessary for that learning module.

When all the questions were discussed, Steve explained the project to the class. The project was designed so that students could demonstrate that they could apply the information from the reading material to real-life situations. He asked the students to write up a job order for their work that reflected the way construction specifications were written for a real construction job. In Figure 5.3, the reader can see what Steve required the students to develop through their writing experience. His rationale for requiring the written work was twofold.

Figure 5.3   Writing Job Specifications

LESSON ON DEVELOPING JOB SPECIFICATIONS FOR WALL FRAMING WITH WOOD	
Job Expectation	*Detail*
Is this a load- or nonload-bearing wall?	(Name the type of wall.)
How was the type of wall determined?	(Explain how the type of wall was determined.)
Is the layout on deck or foundation?	(State where layout is placed.)
What must be done for layout?	(Explain detail for the respective type of layout.)
What is the layout detail?	(Offer step-by-step detail. All details must be in sentence form with clear descriptions. Remember that details must be explicit when it comes to dimensions and construction codes.) 1. 2. 3. 4. 5.

Source: Developed by Steve Younkers.

First, he emphasized to students that written job specifications are part of the legal contract between the contractor and the person requesting the work and are used frequently in this industry. Therefore, it was important for the students to learn to develop written specifications. Second, Steve noticed an increase in student comprehension since he began to require students to develop the written job specifications, so he continued to do so.

Steve wanted students to refer to the textbook material and the construction code book as they wrote their job specifications. He explained that good carpenters refer to written material all the time when developing specifications. He also wanted students to refer to the material that they had read because it would help them solidify their understanding of the textual material they were learning.

Requiring writing to help the student comprehend is scary when we consider that students often struggle with writing. Sharples (2003) indicated that writing is a painful experience because the writer must delve deeply into his own intellect in order to synthesize thoughts. However, writing is significantly related to the success students will have with learning (Schmoker, 2007b). Schmoker also submitted that writing is thinking in its most powerful form.

Kristie Buell, a social studies teacher in the regular high school where we piloted this program, used writing in postreading and learning experiences all the time. One place where she said the writing has been particularly effective came in a thematic unit based on the 2002 Quecreek mining disaster that occurred in Pennsylvania. Kristie said,

> If I simply assigned a report at the end of the unit, the students would reject the idea and complain. I find that when I take them through the pre-reading, during-reading process first, the students are motivated to develop written reports based on their understanding of what they have done prior to writing. (Kristie Buell, personal communication)

Since this high school lies in a small Pennsylvania community with a mining heritage, Kristie used local history to help students understand the impact of America's industrial movement. She believed that the most effective way to help students understand the difficult lives that people lived in the late nineteenth century and during the first half of the twentieth century was to have the students use their current knowledge in connection with the past. The Quecreek mining incident occurred within seventy-five miles of this high school, and most of the students were fully aware of what happened when the miners were trapped in the mine because of the local media's constant attention to the situation.

Kristie started the Quecreek unit by having students work in groups and share information they remembered about the mining accident. She stimulated them with one question for the entire class, "Who in this class remembers the mining accident that occurred in Somerset County a couple of years ago?" This question was used to determine how many students recalled details of the incident. From her pre-assessment, she decided which students would be assigned to what groups to discuss the memories. She tried very hard to make sure that each group had students who had clear memories of the accident teamed with students who either reacted slowly to her large-group question or indicated that they had no memory of Quecreek.

Kristie directed the groups to discuss the following four questions:

1. Did you have any family or friends involved in any aspect of the accident and what did they tell you?

2. What do you remember about the accident?

3. What do you remember about the news coverage of the accident?

4. What questions do you have about the mining accident?

While the students discussed the four questions, each student kept his or her own notes. Kristie picked one person from each group to report what the group was discussing and what questions they had. All students had to be ready to report on what the group discussed and state the group's questions because the students did not know who would be called upon to offer information to the class.

As each group reported their knowledge and posed questions that they had about the accident, Kristie listed the questions on her whiteboard in front of the room. When each of the groups had reported, Kristie handed the students a sheet of paper with numbers and spaces (see the sheet in Figure 5.4). She told the students to write the questions shown on the front board in the spaces provided on the sheet. After students had done this, Kristie orally gave the students some other questions she thought would be helpful when the students viewed a DVD account of the Quecreek accident. She required that they write these questions as she posed them.

During the DVD viewing, the students were expected to provide information on the questions from the prelearning activity

Figure 5.4　Directed-Viewing Question Template

LESSON ON MINING ACCIDENTS
Question 1:   Answer or explanation for Question 1:
Question 2:   Answer or explanation for Question 2:
Question 3:   Answer or explanation for Question 3:
Question 4:   Answer or explanation for Question 4:

Source: Developed by Kristie Buell.

(see Figure 5.4). These questions replicated the model of the directed-reading questions used with reading assignments. The directed-viewing questions engaged the students in interacting with the information from the DVD.

After the viewing, Kristie placed the students into groups again. She told them that after their small-group discussion, they would write five complete sentences to state what they learned about the Quecreek accident. In the groups, the students discussed the responses that they had developed for directed-viewing questions. She reminded them to keep some notes so they could write five sentences about their learning. When group discussions came to an end, Kristie directed the students to individually write five sentences.

All of this activity was only the precursor to what Kristie was leading the students to do in relation to the historical relevance of mining to the industrial growth of America. After Kristie reviewed the five sentences that each student had written, she informed the class of their next assignment, a written report. She placed the class in groups of three and told them that everything they had learned about Quecreek would be very important to their major assignment.

Kristie assigned each group of three students to find information about any coal mine accident that occurred between 1885 and 1945 using library and Internet resources. She told the students that they would write a report to compare and contrast the Quecreek accident to the accident that they chose to research. She told students that the report had to compare and contrast the following six ideas:

1. What are the details about how the researched mine accident occurred?

2. Where did the researched accident occur and what are the details about the community where it occurred?

3. How was the Quecreek mine accident different from the mine accident that was researched?

4. How was the Quecreek mine accident like the mine accident that was researched?

5. What did the government do after the researched accident?

6. What did the government do after the Quecreek accident?

The final directions Kristie gave to the students were given to assure accountability of all group participants. She informed the students that each group member must write the answers to two of the questions. The group's final report had to be divided into six sections and each section would have an individual author who was identified when the report was submitted. She told students that after the report was written, the group would present the report in a PowerPoint presentation to the whole class.

Kristie used a very unique approach to accomplish both the reports and the teaching. Each day students gave her accounts of what they were learning about their researched mine accident. As they gave their accounts, Kristie asked the students if they knew what was happening in the country and the world at the time of the mine accident. She then proceeded to provide direct instruction about the time period. For example, if one set of students said they were studying a mine disaster that occurred in 1917, Kristie offered direct instruction about World War I and its impact on industrial growth in the United States. She used the mine disaster research as the backdrop to opening the thoughts and questions about specific times and events in industrial history.

This lesson and its historical outgrowth were quite sophisticated, but the concepts of the postreading were also very relevant. The students used a common experience to stimulate their thinking. Kristie used questions to keep the students engaged during the viewing of a DVD. She also used further questions to stimulate the development of the report. Finally, she required students to use writing to solidify their knowledge and comprehension of mining and history. She used writing after a learning experience to extend student learning.

In this chapter, we looked at different ways that actively involving students in activities after a reading or learning experience extends and enhances the learning. These activities move students into applying information gained from a learning experience or a reading experience. Schmoker (2006) strongly supported the concept of bringing reading and writing together. He used this statement from Richard Paul (as cited in Sparks, 2005) to substantiate his belief: "Only when students can articulate in writing the basic principles they are learning . . . can we be sure that they are internalizing those principles in an intellectually coherent way" (p. xvii).

6

Putting It All Together

$\mathbf{C}$heri Long teaches mathematics with a focus on literacy skills. She recognizes that students cannot fully comprehend math unless they have mastered certain vocabulary and can communicate effectively using math terminology. When we visited with Cheri, she emphasized that all of her instructional units included vocabulary development and group discussion about the concepts she wanted the students to learn. She pointed out that the discussion and the vocabulary development helped students to share information in a commonly understood language.

Cheri demonstrated this in a lesson on analyzing a set of graphs and a set of statements. She started the lesson by breaking the students into small groups. Each group was asked to view a set of algebraic statements and a set of graphs. The group worked together to categorize the algebraic statements as linear equations and inequalities, systems of equations and inequalities, quadratic equations, or inequalities. Each small group also did the same with the group of graphs on which they were focused.

The teacher's purpose in this activity was to have students discuss terminology and graphic information prior to the delivery of instruction. When the groups finished their categorization, Cheri had each group share what they did and report how and why they categorized the terms and graphs as they did. While each group presented, Cheri wrote key vocabulary words on the board without stopping the presentations to define the terms. At that point, she just wanted the words in front of the class. Some of the words were words that the students used in their discussion. Others were words that occurred to Cheri as the students presented; they said things that triggered a thought in Cheri's mind about a key word she wanted to highlight, and when that happened, she wrote that term on the board even though the students may not have stated it directly.

When the groups completed giving their reports to the entire class, Cheri asked the students to copy the list of words from the board. She then began direct instruction about the different types of graphs for one-variable and two-variable linear equations. She went on to talk about the difference between the graphs of an equation and an inequality. Further, she told the students about the differences between a linear graph, a quadratic graph, and an exponential graph. Finally, she explained the difference between the graph of a single equation or inequality and the graph of a system of equations or inequalities.

While she lectured about these differences, she told the students that when she mentioned one of the words on the list they had copied, they should place a check mark beside the word. She also told them that when she said something that connected to one of their categorized groups, they should make a notation about it on their categorized listing.

Cheri's purpose was twofold: (1) she wanted students to focus on her very brief lecture with some background knowledge and (2) she wanted to begin making connections with words and the work the students did at the start of the lesson. As Cheri talked, the students listened intently for her use of the words on the list, which heightened their awareness of important vocabulary and concepts. When she completed her brief direct instruction for this lesson, she told the students to return to their groups and discuss the vocabulary list and the categories of graphs and equations they had developed. She told them that there were no right or wrong answers, but that they were supposed to make hypotheses as to whether their categorized lists were correct and make inferences as to the meanings of the words on their lists. In effect, Cheri used prelearning, during-learning, and postlearning activities all within about twenty-five minutes.

Students Today

We are not suggesting that everything with this teaching/learning approach can be done in one lesson, and we are not suggesting that all the strategies are extremely brief activities. Instead, we are showing that teachers *can* use several of these strategies within one lesson and that many of the strategies *do* involve brief periods of time to meet the needs of today's students. This short time for activities is critical in the twenty-first century. Students today are used to rapid-fire activities and expect quick, multiple opportunities for learning. We must recognize that students want to engage in brief activities that have a clear purpose. According to Prensky (2001), today's students are *digital natives*—they have grown up using computers, digital devices, and games as part of their everyday life. Because of this, these digital natives expect quick responses, and they expect to spend little time finding information. After all, they can Google a term and find information about that term along with pictures and further connections almost instantaneously.

Prensky (2004) described today's students as a generation that is strong in taking in information and making decisions quickly. They are better at multitasking and parallel processing than previous generations. They are a generation that thinks graphically rather than textually. The students of today assume connectivity, and they see the world through games and cell phones. Foreman (2003) held that students expect immediate feedback, explorative learning environments, and enduring conceptual structures. We believe the strategies outlined in this book offer the type of opportunities that both Prensky and Foreman see as a way of connecting to the digital native. Moving students from an individual activity, to a small-group activity, to a whole-class sharing provides opportunities to learn in a variety of ways and in a variety of contexts. In addition, the focus on before, during, and after reading provides students with a structure that will engage their thinking when approaching new information found in any format.

Today's digital natives still need to learn to read print as well as digital material in order to meet the demands of the information world. Students need to learn how to manage text whether it be online or in a book. They need to practice prelearning techniques, during-learning techniques, and postlearning techniques regardless of what they are going to read or graphically analyze. The goal of this kind of instruction is that students will continue to use these practices independently when reading. Effective, experienced readers of informational text in any format think about the genre and format they will read and activate the background knowledge they have on that topic before beginning to read. They also think while they read to remember, infer, question, confirm, analyze, and critique. After reading, they take time to think about what they have read in a way that makes it their own or they talk with others about what they have read to add to their learning.

Prensky's (2001) digital natives must know how to navigate information in order to establish a basis for acquiring knowledge and developing strong understanding in order to better comprehend. This process helps students do exactly that. By following the methodology from the previous chapters, teachers will help students garner the ability to find information, process information, and comprehend information.

In this book, we have attempted to provide an instructional framework for secondary teachers that will not only help students learn the content being taught in the classroom but will also improve their reading ability in a variety of texts. By engaging students in brief activities before, during, and after learning, students are provided with support for remembering content knowledge as well as a model for approaching any text. At the same time, we are advocating for the instructional techniques that meet today's students. Learning is done through questioning, directed activity, and group processing. These are the kinds of things that students today know and understand.

In addition to learning the content knowledge required in each subject area, students are learning strategies that will help them with anything they read in the future. In this way, the lesson activities and procedures become more than just something that is done during a specific class for a grade. The activities lead students to actions they can take whenever they are reading anything. Since these learning events are designed as short experiences, students are learning to read within the model that fits with today's wired generation.

Following Through With Assessment

As part of the process for determining the effectiveness of teaching practices, it is critical for a school, a department, and individual teachers to make decisions about what data will serve as measures of student achievement (Stiggins, 2005). Standardized test scores, such as those from state assessments, are one gauge of student achievement. These assessments are important indicators of achievement and are also important in working to meet the requirements of the No Child Left Behind Act. As will be seen in the Appendix, the schools involved in using the literacy practices described in this book made gains in scores on state assessments. These assessments continue to show gains in reading scores over time for the school as a whole and can indicate that changes in instructional practices are making a difference in student reading achievement.

However, standardized tests are only given once a year and teachers and schools need other measures of achievement to show student growth at various times throughout the school year and in all subject areas (Stiggins, 2005). Table 6.1 highlights some of the formal and informal assessments that teachers can use to measure student learning and student growth. Teachers can analyze unit tests or daily classroom work as a measure of student achievement more frequently than would be possible if only standardized test data were used. When classroom assessments are analyzed on a more frequent basis, teachers can see improvements, however small they may be, in student learning. These types of informal assessments provide information on how students are improving over time in their learning within the school year, and if baseline information has been set in previous years, how students are improving over time. In addition to serving as a motivational factor for teachers and students, assessments can be used to make instructional decisions for classroom teaching and for working with individual students.

Table 6.1   Assessment

Formal Assessments:	*Informal Assessments:*
Assessments that have a standard form of measurement used to compare achievement between students and compare achievement for one student over time.	*Assessments that are based on the professional judgment of the teacher in determining the gains, progress, or needs of the student.*
• Textbook tests • Rubrics • Final projects • Inventories • Achievement tests (norm referenced, criterion referenced, and/or performance-based tests required by the school, district, or state)	• Teacher-made tests • Interviews • Self-evaluations • Surveys (with students and parents) • Observations • Conferences (with students and parents) • Reflections (oral and written) • Exit slips

Source: Adapted from Mahurt, Metcalfe, & Gwyther, 2007.

For example, in a history classroom, one teacher usually planned units of study around different eras in American history. In the past, she used a series of written tests to measure student learning in each unit. She kept data on how many students passed these assessments for the last two years because she felt that fewer students were passing the tests. Her data showed her that the number of students passing the unit tests remained about the same—75%. Although test scores weren't declining, she wasn't satisfied with the results. She wanted more students passing tests as evidence that more students were learning class content.

This teacher began using the teaching methods from this book to see if they would make a difference in student learning; after the first unit test, 84% of the students had passed the test. She felt that her new instructional practices could have made a difference in improved student achievement in history and was motivated to continue to try the new practices and to collect data. As student scores on class tests improved, the motivation to continue the new instructional approaches propelled the teacher forward. She wanted to improve achievement through changes in instruction and was able to collect evidence that what she was doing made a difference for student learning.

What Does This Mean for Teachers?

It is important for teachers who want to improve student achievement through improving instruction to work within their schools to put several things in place. First, schools must have a vision and direction for the process, and schools need to create mechanisms for developing reflective practice, either through the formal coaching process with a designated coach or through a peer-reflection process.

Second, having the opportunity to meet and discuss aspects of instruction with others is extremely important. Study-group discussions of readings on effective instructional methods as well as discussions on issues and concerns about those methods are needed as teachers begin to implement them. In addition to discussions, teachers should analyze lessons together with questions such as, What did the students learn from this lesson? How do we know they learned it? What aspects of the lesson made it effective for student learning? How were the students engaged during the lesson? How did students' work today allow them to work from a scientist's perspective, a social scientist's perspective, as a mathematician, and so on? How was the lesson structured to provide scaffolded support before, during, and after reading? Discussions and lesson analysis can take place in large-group faculty meetings, department meetings, special mentoring groupings, book study-group meetings, or informal colleague discussions. Individual teachers can work with a trusted colleague to begin these critical reflective processes.

Improving Content Learning and Literacy

We have demonstrated a process teachers can use to facilitate student learning in content areas as well as develop student literacy abilities. This book provides a lesson framework that includes activities before, during, and after learning. We feel this process is one that teachers can use effectively and efficiently. The process involves not only improved learning in content subject areas but also improved reading ability—in particular, improved vocabulary and comprehension. This approach means that time spent in the content classroom will serve two purposes—helping students learn and helping students become more competent readers.

In this book, we have advised that teachers provide opportunities for students to engage in activities before, during, and after learning in order to improve student ability to understand content knowledge and to improve reading comprehension strategies. Since instruction in secondary schools often focuses on a transmission model with the goal of covering a range of material, maintaining order, and working within the time constraints of class periods (Alvermann, 2001), it is important that teachers see how involving students in the learning process actively, rather than as a passive listener or reader, can allow for more effective learning. Following the processes in this book can lead to higher levels of student engagement that can help maintain order. This can provide for increased learning of content information, as well as reading comprehension, and can be done within the typical time constraints of secondary schools.

Appendix

School Examples Using
Instructional Framework

This book grew from initial work in two high schools that faced
the challenge presented by low reading scores. One of the
schools is a vocational-technical school that offers a full academic
program in conjunction with a technical program. Students in this
school can take traditional academic courses and prepare to achieve
a level of certification in one of seventeen technical programs. The
other school is a small, traditional high school housing grades seven
through twelve. This high school traditionally scores well in reading,
but the principal believed the improved teaching techniques would
benefit all of his teachers regardless of academic curriculum.

Both schools went through the same professional-development
training to improve literacy through their work in content-area instruction. Reading was seen as a primary source of new information and
learning in each of these schools. Therefore, reading was considered
an essential skill in learning any content regardless of the discipline.
The professional-development training emphasized that many high
school students are reluctant readers who sometimes lack the strategies
necessary to use reading material for learning. The training emphasized that students need language-rich learning environments no
matter what their reading ability (Sturtevant, 2003).

There were several specific points presented to teachers throughout
the professional-development process. First, the teachers were told,
"You are not a reading teacher unless you are certified as a reading
teacher." Knowing that many secondary content teachers can be

irritated by the phrases "reading across the curriculum" and "all teachers are teachers of reading," the professional development stayed away from emphasizing that teachers should teach reading skills. Second, an emphasis was placed on the fact that while many high school students have reading difficulty, few secondary students could be considered nonreaders. Third, teachers were told that if they engaged students in certain reading activities, the students would comprehend more of the information related to the subjects being taught. The teachers were told that the literacy instruction system was designed to help students become more engaged in learning activities and therefore create higher levels of student comprehension in their respective subjects. The fourth point put an emphasis on the importance of reading in the twenty-first-century workplace. Teachers were reminded that by requiring students to engage in textual material, students were given a far better opportunity for developing the skills necessary to meet the expectations of the work world (Casner-Lotto & Barrington, 2006).

Issues in a Vocational-Technical School

A specific example of the need for high-level reading and problem solving in the workplace surfaced when we studied the comprehensive technical high school where we first piloted our performance literacy program. The school's executive director wanted to know if students were achieving mastery of the skills that the businesses and industries in the area wanted. He was particularly concerned that the No Child Left Behind (NCLB) requirements were leading away from preparing quality technicians who knew and could do the technical tasks required in the workplace. He was concerned that teachers were torn between focusing their instructional time on preparing students for the state tests in reading and math and preparing students for the technical skills needed in the workforce.

In years prior to our involvement, the school started to move away from the "technical academic" courses, such as "technical math" or "technical English," to a more traditional college preparatory program where courses such as trigonometry and college algebra, physics, and college-preparatory English became the norm for many of the students. The impetus for moving to the more traditional academic course offerings came about in the late 1990s and early 2000s as a result of the Secretary's Commission on Achieving Necessary Skills (SCANS) Report (1991) and NCLB regulations. The school realized that the workplace would require not only knowledge but analysis of how to use the appropriate knowledge in critical situations. The school leaders realized that in order for students to apply knowledge, they would have to develop students who could read and think about more complex material.

Following the view that increasing rigor meant enrolling students in challenging academic courses, the school staff determined that higher-level courses would develop higher-achieving students. The assumption was that a more academic curriculum would raise the bar for all students and that the test scores in the academic areas would improve, while at the same time the technical test scores would remain stable or increase because students would become better readers and stronger mathematics students. There is evidence that such a concept might work. According to Toch, Jerald, and Dillon (2007), low-achieving students do not appear to suffer from taking tough, college-prep courses. Their evidence indicates that a combination of rigor, relevance, and good instruction can lead to higher student achievement. In addition, they report that enrollment in career and technical education is positively associated with higher graduation rates—but only when technical courses are taken along with challenging academic courses. The school also had evidence that academic test scores were increasing as all students were shifting to a traditional college preparatory academic curriculum. Figure A.1 shows how the state test scores in reading increased from 1995 until 2003. Obviously, the school was doing something that was helping students increase their academic skills in reading.

Figure A.1   Pennsylvania System of School Assessment Reading Scores for Vocational-Technical School

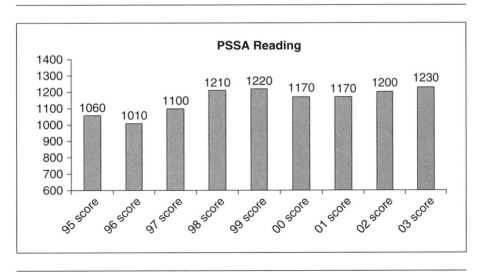

Source: Columbia-Montour Area Vocational-Technical School Administration and Faculty.

Even with this growth of almost two hundred points from 1995 to 2003, the school was not reaching the Annual Yearly Progress (AYP) scores required under NCLB, as seen in Table A.1. By 2004, the school was in School Improvement 1 and needed to develop a plan to attack reading scores. The director and the administrative team wanted the school to demonstrate academic success and help students achieve the scores necessary for making AYP. In addition to the test results, the school leaders wanted to conduct a study to help them understand if technical readiness and meeting NCLB requirements were equal in their importance to the business community they served.

The school's director knew that the local businesses and local technical advisory boards expected his school to develop work-ready graduates who could enter the workplace upon completion of their school career. He also knew that if the school did not raise reading scores, there would be continual bad publicity about the school's test scores and students might not achieve at their highest levels. He contacted us to perform a study to provide information that would help define a way to increase test scores or provide evidence that the school was meeting these challenges.

The research question was "Is this school completing its mission?" The school's mission was *Business, Industry, and Community: Preparing Students to Meet the Challenges of Work and Life in an Ever Changing World*. The director was very concerned that demands for academic rigor had fragmented his school into the technical education side and the academic education side. The director indicated that he believed that the technical side was most important from the perspective of the

Table A.1   Pennsylvania System of School Assessment Reading Scoring Quadrant Groups From 2001 Through 2004

Year	Percent Advanced Proficient	Percent Proficient	Percent Basic	Percent Below Basic
2001	1.3	29.4	30.1	39.2
2002	2.9	30.7	29.3	37.1
2003	4.1	33.7	32	30.2
2004	6.7	30.9	25.5	36.9

Source: Columbia-Montour Area Vocational-Technical School Administration and Faculty.

community. He felt that the major question of employers was, "Can this student work for us?"

The results of the study indicated that he was correct in his thinking, but not quite to the level that he had thought. The study concluded that most people within the school's boundaries believed that the school was doing a good job (Perna, 2004). Few individual reactions of employers, parents, and students rated the school below a 3.0 on a 5.0 scale. The vast majority of scores concerning competency were in the 4.0 to 5.0 range. Interestingly, the businesspeople supported the conclusion of the executive director that job skills were more of a focus than mathematics, reading, and writing test scores. Table A.2 shows the average point value of each statement in a series of questions about what businesspeople thought the focus of the school should be. The reader can see that work skills and technical testing are more important to the businesspeople than academic testing. However, the businesspeople showed that reading test scores were an important aspect of the students' training. Fifteen of the twenty-five businesspeople

Table A.2 Business Responses to Statements About Testing and Workplace Skills

Likert Scale: 1 is *Not Important* and 5 is *Very Important*   *n* = 25

Statement	*Average Rating*
The school should focus on being certain that students score proficient scores on the state tests in reading.	3.88
The school should focus on being certain that students score proficient scores on the state tests in math.	3.76
The school should focus on being certain that students score proficient scores on the state tests in writing.	3.64
The school should focus on being certain that students are able to pass tests that certify them in specific technical careers.	4.84
The school should focus on being certain that students develop workplace skills.	4.96

Source: Columbia-Montour Area Vocational-Technical School Administration and Faculty.

rated reading scores as 4.0 or 5.0 on the scale. This led us to conclude that they saw reading as a significant skill. Beyond evidence found in the questions shown in Table A.2, there was strong evidence that reading was important in a series of open-ended questions that focused on thoughts about the school's preparation of future employees. The heart of the questions dealt with the needs and expectations of people who started to work for the respective businesses.

When responding to what they expected and what the school needed to teach, the business owners and managers unequivocally said that reading and procedural thinking were necessary for successful employment. The businesspeople and industry people made it clear that the school should focus on developing students who could search for solutions in written material and follow the steps outlined in textual documents. For example, the electric utilities representatives from a nuclear power plant said that all employees had to refer to the procedural and policy manuals at all times. The manuals provided written information that outlined the procedures that employees are required to follow in order to complete any task in the plant.

The businesspeople saw technical work skills as an important verification that the school was doing what it was supposed to do. However, when talking about what they needed and expected in new employees, the word *reading* kept surfacing. The businesses wanted the school to prepare students who could read and apply what they had read to complete a work task.

From other information in the study, there was evidence that students were not seeing the connection between reading and technical work programs. Seniors in the school were asked if they had been shown how reading was related to their chosen technical program. Only 21 of the 131 seniors said that they had been shown that reading was directly connected to their chosen technical program, and 53 seniors indicated that they were not shown how reading was connected to their future work (Perna, 2004).

Beyond the idea of connecting reading to specific technical careers, the study uncovered another issue related to the division between academic and technical programs. Nineteen of twenty-seven academic teachers said that they seldom if ever assigned reading outside of class time. Nine of thirteen technical teachers said that they did not assign reading outside of class time (Perna, 2004). Teachers may not have been encouraging students to read as a part of the academic or technical training.

The open-ended reaction to questions gave some explanation as to why the teachers had not emphasized reading in connection to career or as assigned learning experiences. The study showed that teachers did not assign reading because students were not completing the reading when it was assigned (Perna, 2004). The second point made by both academic and technical teachers was that the students did not have the skills to read the type of material that they wanted them to read. A third reason as to why teachers did not assign reading out of class was that many of the students worked after school and it was assumed that they did not have time to read.

When the director and the administrative staff held meetings to discuss the findings of the study, they targeted their conclusions both on the need to help teachers make connections between reading and technical learning and the need to encourage teachers to make certain that students were reading. They sought ideas from teachers, students, and other schools. Ultimately, they determined that the school's theme for the 2004–2005 school year would be "Reading Is a Work Skill."

The administrative team determined that this theme would be the start of a campaign that could bring both sides of the school together and also be a sounding cry for their school improvement plan. The school's leaders realized that a slogan alone could not guarantee success with reading scores. Since the school was required to develop a school improvement plan for reading, the director worked with us to use data and information from the school study to create a professional development program that would help enhance the use of reading and instruction related to reading. As the plan evolved, the administrators used the school theme as a way to invoke help from all teachers—not just the teachers of English and reading who worked with literacy as a central theme of their curriculum.

As we worked with the director and his administrative staff to develop an instructional concept that would help students become stronger thinkers and readers, we kept noting that good readers followed a process. They used prereading activities that engaged them in calling up what they knew prior to reading. They used during-reading activities that caused them to interact with the written material. They also used postreading activities that solidified what they learned during reading.

To provide the teachers with a system that employed the three steps in reading, a discussion between school administrators and our consulting group was held. All people agreed that the study with the business community had clearly indicated a need for emphasis on procedural behaviors as well as reading and writing skills. The decision was made to develop a collaborative way to help students learn a procedure while enhancing the opportunity for greater learning comprehension. Our group suggested that students had to learn processes for reading, writing, and listening in order to effectively use these skills in learning. We contended that to comprehend at the highest levels, students needed to be engaged in the material that they were to learn.

The school leaders decided to offer a series of professional-development workshops that would help teachers begin using pre-reading, during reading, and postreading activities, regardless of the subject they taught. School administrators and the consulting team agreed that this process would provide teachers with strategies to increase student engagement in learning activities. Instead of teachers acting as deliverers of information, the teachers would become facilitators of procedural steps that would lead students to active engagement in learning. Students would do the work of learning, and teachers would guide the students to move through the procedure for learning.

Initial Professional Development

The professional-development plan was designed so that teachers and all administrators would see how pre-, during-, and postliteracy activities could become commonplace in instruction.

At first, *Procedural Literacy* was the key term we used to identify the process that teachers would use to facilitate students becoming more highly engaged in reading and learning. The process followed the basic concepts found in much of the literature about successful reading. Successful readers utilize prereading activities to connect what they already know to what they will read. Successful readers pose their own questions and thoughts about what they are reading as they read the material. Successful readers act on what they have read after reading in order to develop comprehension of the material.

The series of workshops in both schools were similar. We required that administrators be part of the process, as is emphasized by the National Staff Development Council (NSDC, 2001). Also following the NSDC model, we broke the faculties into small learning communities and created a series of professional-development sessions. The professional-development sessions were broken into training days, followed by several days of practical implementation, and then more training sessions. This methodology provided teachers with the opportunity to implement some concepts and then return to training with questions, comments, and concerns about the instructional strategies.

We began the professional development by emphasizing that all teachers are not teachers of reading, but that all teachers used some form of reading and writing as part of their instruction and used the information on the teacher's role.

The Teacher's Role

- A reading teacher teaches students how to read, *but* all teachers can help students read effectively.

- A reading teacher can measure and determine a student's reading skill, *but* all teachers can offer students an opportunity to develop the reading skill.

- English teachers can teach students how to write, *but* all teachers can offer students an opportunity to write.

Measures of Success

The two schools mentioned have had success in increasing their state test scores. The technical school has achieved two consecutive years of meeting Annual Yearly Progress. Table A.3 shows how the scores have changed since using before-, during-, and after-reading activities with their students.

Table A.3 Pennsylvania System of School Assessment Reading Scoring Quadrant Groups From 2002 Through 2006

	Percent Advanced Proficient	*Percent Proficient*	*Percent Basic*	*Percent Below Basic*
2002	2.9	30.7	29.3	37.1
2003	4.1	33.7	32.0	30.2
2004	6.7	30.9	25.5	36.9
2005	16.4	37.0	22.4	24.2
2006	9.5	34.8	29.1	26.9

Source: Columbia-Montour Area Vocational-Technical School Administration and Faculty.

The fact that the school achieved AYP for two successive years is important. However, a more important indicator may demonstrate the power of using these instructional strategies. This technical school has a significant population of special-education students. Since the school has implemented this instructional process, they have seen a growth in the reading scores of special-education students. The school tracks the scores of students from eighth grade and at the technical school, and 31% of the students with special needs have moved from *basic* and *below basic* as eighth graders to *advanced proficient* or *proficient* readers as eleventh graders.

The regular high school has also seen a rise in test scores since implementing the program. As stated, the school had test scores above the AYP mark for several years. However, during the year that the teachers in the school were going through their training process, only 47.4% of the eleventh-grade students achieved the *advanced proficient* or *proficient* rating in reading. The school focused on use of the system in the 2006–2007 school term, and that year 60.67% of the students reached the advanced proficient and proficient range. Thus, there is evidence that when secondary teachers use a set of instructional procedures for guiding students' text reading, student achievement improves.

References

Alexander, P. (2005/2006). The path to competence: A lifespan developmental perspective on reading. *Journal of Literacy Research, 37,* 413–436.

Allington, R. (1995). *No quick fix: Rethinking literacy in America's elementary schools.* New York: Teachers College Press.

Allington, R. L. (2001). *What really matters for struggling readers.* New York: Addison-Wesley.

Alvermann, D. E. (2001). *Effective literacy instruction for adolescents.* Paper and executive summary commissioned by the National Reading Conference, Chicago, IL. Retrieved April 10, 2006, from http://www.nrconline.org/publications/alverwhite2.pdf

Anderson, R. C., Spiro, R. J., & Anderson, M. C. (1978). Schemata as scaffolding for the representation of information in connected discourse. *American Educational Research Journal, 15,* 433–440.

Balfanz, R., McPartland, J., & Shaw, A. (2002). *Re-conceptualizing extra help for high school students in a high standards era.* Paper presented at the Preparing for America's Future High School Symposium, Office of Adult and Vocational Education, U.S. Department of Education, Washington, D.C.

Beers, K. (2003). *When kids can't read: What teachers can do.* Portsmouth, NH: Heinemann.

Beuhl, D. (n.d.). *Literacy and sound learning: Strategies for thoughtful reading.* Retrieved September 1, 2007, from http://soundlearning.publicradio.org/standard/docs/reading_strategies.shtml

Biancarosa, G., & Snow, C. (2004). *Reading next: A vision for action and research in middle and secondary school—A report to Carnegie Corporation of New York* (2nd ed.). Washington, DC: Alliance for Excellent Education.

Casner-Lotto, J., & Barrington, L. (2006). *Are they really ready to work? Employers' perspectives on the basic knowledge and applied skills of new entrants to the 21st century US workforce.* New York: The Conference Board.

Daniels, H., & Zemelman, S. (2004). *Subjects matter: Every teacher's guide to content-area reading.* Portsmouth, NH: Heinemann.

Duke, N. (2006, July). *Of head lice and helicopters: Engaging and effective informational literacy instruction.* Paper presented at the Purdue Literacy Network Project Summer Literacy Institute, West Lafayette, IN.

Duke, N. K., & Pearson, P. D. (2002). Effective practices for developing reading comprehension. In A. Farstrup & S. J. Samuels (Eds.), *What research has to say about reading instruction* (pp. 205–242). Newark, DE: International Reading Association.

Dymock, S. (2005). Teaching expository text structure awareness. *The Reading Teacher, 59*(2), 177–181.

Elbow, P. (1994). *Writing for learning—Not just for demonstrating learning.* Amherst, MA: University of Massachusetts. Retrieved October 12, 2007, from http://www.ntlf.com/html/lib/bib/writing.htm

Fisher, D., & Frey, N. (2007). *Checking for understanding: Formative assessment techniques for your classroom.* Alexandria, VA: Association for Supervision and Curriculum Development.

Foreman, J. (2003, July/August). Next generation: Educational technology versus the lecture. *EduCause Review*, 12–22. Retrieved August 4, 2008, from http://net.educause.edu/ir/library/pdf/erm0340.pdf

Fountas, I. C., & Pinnell, G. S. (2001). *Guiding readers and writers: Grades 3–6.* Portsmouth, NH: Heinemann.

Friedman, T. (2006). *The world is flat.* New York: Farrar, Straus, & Giroux.

Fritz, J. (1997). *Shh! We're writing the constitution.* New York: G. P. Putnam.

Graham, S., & Perin, D. (2007). *Writing next: Effective strategies to improve writing of adolescents in middle and high schools—A report to Carnegie Corporation of New York.* Washington, DC: Alliance for Excellent Education.

Guthrie, J. T., & Wigfield, A. (2000). Engagement and motivation in reading. In M. L. Kamil, P. B. Mosenthal, P. D. Pearson, & R. Barr (Eds.), *Handbook of reading research,* Vol. 3 (pp. 403–422). Mahwah, NJ: Erlbaum.

Harvey, S., & Goudvis, A. (2007). *Strategies that work: Teaching comprehension for understanding and engagement* (2nd ed.). Portland, ME: Stenhouse.

Heller, R., & Greenleaf, C. L. (2007). *Literacy instruction in the content areas: Getting to the core of middle and high school improvement.* Washington, DC: Alliance for Excellent Education.

Jacobs, V. (1999, July/August). What secondary teachers can do to teach reading. *Harvard Education Letter.* Retrieved September 21, 2007, from http://www.edletter.org/past/issues/1999-ja/secondary.shtml

Keene, E. O., & Zimmerman, S. (2007). *Mosaic of thought: The power of comprehension strategy instruction* (2nd ed.). Portsmouth, NH: Heinemann.

Kristo, J. V., & Bamford, R. A. (2004). *Nonfiction in focus.* New York: Scholastic.

Mahurt, S. (2005). Writing is reading. *Indiana Reading Journal, 37*(1), 19–26.

Mahurt, S. F., Metcalfe, R. E., & Gwyther, M. A. (2007). *Building bridges from early to intermediate literacy.* Thousand Oaks, CA: Corwin.

Marzano, R. (2007). *The art and science of teaching.* Alexandria, VA: Association for Supervision and Curriculum Development.

McConachie, S., Hall, M., Resnick, L., Ravi, A. K., Bill, V. L., Bintz, J., & Taylor, J. A. (2006). Task, text, and talk: Literacy for all subjects. *Educational Leadership, 64*(2), 8–14.

McKenna, M. C., & Robinson, R. D. (1997). *Teaching through text* (2nd ed.). New York: Longman.

Meltzer, J., Smith, N. C., & Clark, H. (2001). *Adolescent literacy resources: Linking research and practice.* Providence, RI: The Education Alliance.

Moje, E. B. (2006, March). *Integrating literacy into the secondary school content areas: An enduring problem in enduring institutions.* Retrieved July 9, 2007, from http://www.umich.edu/~govrel/adoles_lit/moje.pdf

Moore, D. W., Bean, T. W., Birdyshaw, D., & Rycik, J.A. (1999). *Adolescent literacy: A position statement for the Commission on Adolescent Literacy of the International Reading Association.* Newark, DE: International Reading Association.

National Association of State Boards of Education (NASBE). (2006). *Reading at risk: The state response to the crisis in adolescent literacy.* Alexandria: VA: Author.

National Center on Education and the Economy (NCEE). (2007). *Tough choices or tough times: The report of the new Commission on the Skills of the American Workforce.* Washington, DC: Author.

National Commission on Writing for America's Families, Schools and Colleges. (2006). *Writing and school reform.* New York: College Board.

National Staff Development Council (NSDC). (2001). *NSDC's standards for staff development.* Retrieved August 27, 2007, from http://www.nsdc.org/standards/index.cfm

Ogle, D. (1986). K-W-L: A teaching model that develops active reading of expository texts. *The Reading Teacher, 39,* 564–570.

Organization for Economic Co-operation and Development (OECD). (2003). *Reading for change: Performance and engagement across countries.*

Palinscar, A., & Brown, A. (1984). Reciprocal teaching of comprehension-fostering and comprehension monitoring activities. *Cognition and Instruction, 1,* 117–175.

Pennsylvania System of School Assessment (PSSA). *PSSA Results.* Retrieved September 1, 2007, from http://www.pde.state.pa.us/a_and_t/cwp/browse.asp?a=3&bc=0&c=27525&a_and_tNav=|633|&a_and_tNav=

Perie, M., Grigg, W. S., & Donahue, P. L. (2005). *The nation's report card: Reading 2005.* Washington, DC: U.S. Department of Education.

Perna, D. (2004). *A third person view of Columbia-Montour Area Vocational-Technical School: A report for the Columbia-Montour Area Vocational-Technical School.* Northumberland, PA: Author.

Perna, D., & Davis, J. (2006). *Aligning standards and curriculum for classroom success* (2nd ed.). Thousand Oaks, CA: Corwin.

Persky, H. R., Daane, M. C., & Jin, Y. (2003). *The nation's report card: Writing 2002.* Washington, DC: U.S. Department of Education.

Prensky, M. (2001). Digital natives, digital immigrants. *On the Horizon, 9*(5), 1–6. Retrieved August 2, 2008, from http://pre2005.flexiblelearning.net.au/projects/resources/Digital_Natives_Digital_Immigrants.pdf

Prensky, M. (2004). *Use their tools! Speak their language!* Retrieved August 2, 2008, from http://www.marcprensky.com/writing/Prensky-Use_Their_Tools_Speak_Their_Language.pdf

RAND Reading Study Group. (2002). *Reading for understanding: Toward an R&D program in reading comprehension.* Santa Monica, CA: RAND Education.

Readance, J. E., Bean, T. W., & Baldwin, R. S. (1998). *Content area literacy: An integrated approach* (6th ed.). Dubuque, IA: Kendall/Hunt.

Schank, R. (n.d.). *Engines for education.* The Institute for Learning Sciences. Retrieved September 21, 2007, from http://www.engines4ed.org/hyperbook/nodes/NODE-67-pg.html

Schmoker, M. (2006). *Results now.* Alexandria, VA: Association for Supervision and Curriculum Development.

Schmoker, M. (2007a). Radically redesigning literacy instruction. *Phi Delta Kappan, 88,* 488–493.

Schmoker, M. (2007b). Reading, writing, and thinking for all. *Educational Leadership, 64,* 63–66.

Sharples, M. (2003). Electronic publication: Writing for the screen. In B. Bruce (Ed.), *Literacy in the Information Age* (pp. 46–58). Newark, DE: International Reading Association.

Simonsen, S. (1996). Identifying and teaching text structures in content area classrooms. In D. Lapp, J. Flood, & N. Farnan (Eds.), *Content area reading and learning: Instructional strategies* (2nd ed., pp. 59–76). Needham Heights, MA: Allyn & Bacon.

Smith, L. (2001). *Implementing the reading—writing connection.* Retrieved July 15, 2007, from http://www.nade.net/documents/SCP98/SCP98.8.pdf

Smolkin, L. R., & Donovan, C. A. (2002). "Oh excellent, excellent question!" Developmental differences and comprehension acquisition. In C. Collins-Block & M. Pressley (Eds.), *Comprehension instruction: Research-based best practices* (pp. 140–157). New York: Guilford.

Sparks, D. (2005). *Leading for results.* Thousand Oaks, CA: Corwin.

Stiggins, R. (2005). *Student involved assessment for learning* (4th ed.). Upper Saddle River, NJ: Pearson.

Strangman, N., & Hall, T. (2004). *Background knowledge.* Wakefield, MA: National Center on Accessing the General Curriculum. Retrieved August 29, 2007, from http://www.cast.org/publications/ncac/ncac_backknowledge.html

Sturtevant, E. G. (2003). *The literacy coach: A key to improving teaching and learning in secondary schools.* Washington, DC: Alliance for Excellent Education. Retrieved August 18, 2007, from http://www.all4ed.org/publications/LiteracyCoach.pdf

Toch, T., Jerald, C. D., & Dillon, E. (2007). Surprise—High school reform is working. *Phi Delta Kappan, 88*(6), 433–437.

Tovani, C. (2000). *I read it but I don't get it: Comprehension strategies for adolescent readers.* Portland, ME: Stenhouse.

Tovani, C. (2004). *Do I really have to teach reading? Content comprehension grades 6–12.* Portland, ME: Stenhouse.

United States Department of Labor. *Secretary's Commission on Achieving Necessary Skills (SCANS) Report.* (1991). Retrieved July 1, 2007, from http://wdr.doleta.gov/SCANS/

Wiggins, G., & McTighe, J. (2005). *Understanding by design* (2nd ed.). Alexandria, VA: Association for Supervision and Curriculum Development.

Willingham, D. (2006, Spring). How knowledge helps. *American Educator.* Retrieved July, 30, 2007, from http://www.aft.org/pubs-reports/american_educator/issues/spring06/willingham.htm

Index

Note: Page references followed by *f* indicate illustration figures; those followed by *t* indicate tables.

CORWIN

A SAGE Company

The Corwin logo—a raven striding across an open book—represents the union of courage and learning. Corwin is committed to improving education for all learners by publishing books and other professional development resources for those serving the field of PreK–12 education. By providing practical, hands-on materials, Corwin continues to carry out the promise of its motto: **"Helping Educators Do Their Work Better."**